Published by:
Empower Your Life Publishing
publishing@gwm.services

Author- **Chayo Briggs**
chayobriggs.com

ISBN # 978-1-7335551-0-4

Your Credit Defines Your Creditability

By *Chayo Briggs*

Disclaimer

The author has made every effort to ensure the accuracy of the information within this book was correct at time of publication. The author does not assume and hereby disclaims any liability to any party for any loss, damage, or disruption caused by errors or omissions, whether such errors or omissions result from accident, negligence, or any other cause.

The information contained within this Book/eBook is strictly for educational purposes. If you wish to apply ideas contained in this Book/eBook, you are taking full responsibility for your actions.

Disclaimer: The Publisher and the Author make no representation or warranties with respect to the accuracy or completeness of the contents of this work and specifically disclaim all warranties for a particular purpose. No warranty may be created or extended by sales or promotional materials. The advice and strategies contained herein may not be suitable for every situation. This work is sold with the understanding that the Publisher is not engaged in rendering legal, accounting, or other professional services. If professional assistance is required, the services of a competent professional person should be sought. Neither the Publisher nor the Author shall be liable for damages arising therefrom.

The fact that an organization or website is referred to in this work as a citation and/or potential source of further information does not mean that the Author or the Publisher endorses the information, the organization, or website it may provide or recommendations it may make. Further, readers should be aware that websites listed in this work may have changed or disappeared between when this work was written and when it is read.

The cases and stories in this book have had details changed to preserve privacy.

Acknowledgments

I would like to express my gratitude to the many people who saw me through this book; to all those who provided support, talked things over, read, wrote, offered comments, allowed me to quote their remarks and assisted in the editing, proofreading and design.

I would like to thank my mother El Dora Bocino Lay, my father Dr. Ervin Briggs Jr., my wife Dina Renae Flynn Briggs and the rest of my family, who supported and encouraged me in spite of all the time it took me away from them. It was a long and difficult journey for them.

My four angels (my daughters) Saleema El-Amin, Kendra J. Wilson, Kathrine Oliva Hough and Samira El-Amin.

I would like to thank Cydney Rax, Shakeena Whitmore, Michelle E. Alford, Regina Littles, Lashana King Corbett, Jamila Jay Choyce for helping me in the selection and editing process.

Thanks to Lizzy McNett, my publisher, who encouraged me to prosper.

Thanks to Abraham Vega Moreno (brother) and Consumer Grounds- without you this book would never have happened.

My grandfather Dr. Ervin Briggs Sr. and grandmother Dorthy English Kaiser, my sisters and brothers Eva Barnes, Tyrone Lay aka. "kilo" (Fruit Town Piru), Chanda M. Kellogg, Wende "Mosley" Winston, Monica Mason, Kellin Mills, Derick Briggs, Leroy Lay 11, Quishawnta Carmelita Mills-Gibson and Ervin Briggs IV. I would like to give a special thanks to Rebecca Sims, RET United States Air Force Major Cowetta Hinant and my graphic designer Panagiotis Lampridis, and the Facebook group members in Briggs & Lay Pro Big Beautiful Women. - Chayo Briggs.

Table of Contents

Disclaimer 3

Acknowledgments... 4

Author Bio 8

Preface... 10

Introduction... 11

Chapter One: Your Credit Profile 12

Chapter Two: What is Credit? 21

    Four Types of Credit.................................... 21

    Why Do You Need Credit?........................... 22

Chapter Three: Side Effects of Bad Credit 25

    What is Debt Collection?............................. 29

    Debt Scams 33

    Bankruptcy.. 44

    Bankruptcy Schedule C............................... 59

Chapter Four: How is Your Credit Score Calculated?...... 64

Chapter Five: Hard and Soft Credit Inquires 82

    Credit inquiries.. 82

Chapter Six: Bank Accounts and Credit Scoring.............. 87

Chapter Seven: Debt vs Income Ratio 93

Chapter Eight: Dealing with Negative Credit Issues 96

Chapter Nine: Credit Report in Minority Environments 117

Chapter Ten: Fixing Your Credit 122

Chapter Eleven: Dispute an Error 145

Chapter Twelve: Identity Theft..................................... 161

Credit Fraud Prevention Kit.. 171

Consumer Resources... 176

History of Credit Bureaus 179

Equifax Inc.. 179

Experian plc 184

TransUnion 191

Glossary 194

References... 219

Author Bio

As a highly successful real estate investor for over seventeen years, Briggs is driven to obtain the highest standards for his clients. His successes as an effective motivational speaker and published author were developed from life experience. Through those exceptional skills he learned the art of passive income. Chayo can assist his clients in procuring their prosperous future, breaking the chains of financial distress.

The basic concepts of credit stability are simple, but most people see these topics as taboo, when in fact they are essential to becoming a successful financially independent individual. We know such issues are daunting, but you may need to borrow money at some point in the future.

Your credit score determines two things that can affect your loan approval. First, lending money entails risk; lenders need to know you are reliable. Second, your credit score determines the terms of your loan.

In today's society, having just an average credit rating may not be enough. Employers are beginning to check credit history to make sure an employee is a good fit. Think of your credit score as a resume, your life history. It paints a clear example of what type of person you are in real life,

"I have over seventeen years' experience in real estate entrepreneurism and life coaching. One of the first topics discussed is a client's credit rating, because it will determine the next course of action."

In today's economy, something simple like getting a place to live requires a credit history report,

"Therefore, I am committed to assisting people in understanding the importance of credit credibility."

Briggs has a great deal of life experience, making him a skilled expert at helping people overcome their credit creditably issues. In return, he is able to establish a solid foundation for his clients to achieve their credit status goals.

Preface

As an author and public speaker my books offer readers inspiration from my own story and help them learn the fundamentals of rebuilding their credit, as well as entrepreneurial and financial skills. I have been in the real estate business for over seventeen years. My company mission is to educate minority communities on the importance of having good credit in today's society. When someone is able to build a positive credit resume, they can easily obtain passive income to increase their financial investments.

Introduction

Your Credit Defines Your Creditability is designed as a pathway to understanding what contributes to an excellent credit rating. We know such issues are daunting, but you may need to borrow money from a lender. We need to understand and learn that the concept of good credit defines our creditability, so we must learn to delete toxic accounts such as collections, inquiries, charge-offs and public records. Therefore, having a good credit score will make the process easier. Your credit score determines two things that can affect your loan approval. First, lending money entails risk, and lenders need to know you are reliable. Second, your credit score determines the terms of your loan.

Briggs understands the key to success comes through life experience; for that reason, he assists clients in procuring their prosperous future, breaking the chains of financial distress.

Chapter One:

Your Credit Profile

(Your Financial Resume)

Creditors deduce creditability from your credit profile. Think of it as your financial resume. For example:

➤ Are you divorced?

➤ Do you owe massive amounts in student debt?

➤ Are medical debts overwhelming your life?

Any one of these items can be deduced from reading your credit history, plus the trail of accounts associated with these events. Public records are fair game for lenders.

Lenders have exact records of any credit transactions you have ever opened or closed. If you defaulted on an account or had any financial hardships, they are all markers on your financial resume. It's essential that you look at your credit in this fashion to ensure regulation.

Be strategic in how you represent yourself in the financial world. A financial resume is the only way lenders can determine the value of loaning your money; like a mortgage or a car loan. Doing things to increase your credit score and being mindful of the situations will appear during a detailed search and surely improve your chances of gaining access to increased future credit.

Most people have a gut feeling about their credit–it's either great, good or bad. But, what is a bad credit score, really? First, it's important to understand that there are many credit scoring models, and each may use a different scale to convey information.

In the lending world, there are assumptions about credit scores and how they fall into different ranges. For example; what score may qualify as bad, or good. Most major credit scoring models follow a 300 to 850 range. While you're looking at a score measured this way, you generally assume anything below 600 is a bad credit score. Below are how the basic credit tiers typically measure:

- ➢ Excellent Credit: 750+
- ➢ Good Credit: 700-749
- ➢ Fair Credit: 650-699
- ➢ Poor Credit: 600-649
- ➢ Bad Credit: below 600

Let's look at what constitutes a bad credit score.

Who Decides if a Credit Score is Bad?

"As mentioned, credit score ranges can vary by model. For example, all FICO scores range between 300 and 850 with 300 being the lowest possible score, while 850 is the highest possible score."

"The range for VantageScore 2.0 credit scores is between 501 and 990, with the higher number representing the strongest score. But its newer version, VantageScore 3.0, has a range of 300 to 850."

Companies that develop credit scores–FICO and VantageScore, for example–do not decide which credit scores are good or bad. Nor do the credit reporting agencies. Instead, it's up to individual lenders and insurance companies to decide which scores demonstrate an acceptable level of risk. Such as;

> ➤ Determining the interest rate charged for a loan, or in the case of an insurance company, the discount offered on an insurance policy.
> ➤ Deciding whether to extend credit, and how much credit to approve, whether to adjust a customer's credit limit, or even to close a risky account.

In a way, there is no such thing as a "bad credit score," since the number itself doesn't mean anything until a lender decides how to use it. In other words, a credit score is only bad when it voids your financial planning, whether that is to refinance a loan, borrow at a low-interest rate, or get the best deal on your auto insurance.

Moreover, what will be considered bad credit by one lender may be perfectly acceptable to another. For example, with many mortgages, the minimum score required may be a 620, while some credit card issuers offering low-rate cards may reject applicants whose scores are lower than, say 680.

Find Out Where You Stand

It's imperative we track our credit reports on a consistent basis. You can check your credit score using any one of several free reporting agencies. My personal favorite is Identity Guard. You'll see your payment history, debt and other factors affecting your score, along with recommendations for steps to improve your credit resume.

The information may include credit offers from lenders who might be willing to offer you credit. Checking your own credit reports and scores does not affect your credit score in any way. You can start taking your credit score from bad to good by disputing errors on your credit report, paying down excessively high debts and limiting new credit inquiries.

Access to financial services and credit is generally regarded as a necessity to lead a normal life. Just the ability to get a basic bank or savings account requires a stable credit resume. We have not even mentioned mortgages, car loans, or business financial assistance. These are some essential components of our modern economic life.

Yet, financial exclusion–the inability to access these financial services–is a problem for many people. Research has shown that certain groups of society are affected more than others. There are two main areas of financial loans that are accessed the most: consumer credit and mortgages. In both areas, there is evidence to show that ethnic minorities have a difficult time ensuring loans due to poor credit resumes.

Financial barring plays an important role in increasing poverty and limiting prosperity. The link to access wealth is a simple one. It enables spending that exceeds our monthly budgets and gives us the ability to stretch the cost of big purchases over time. Credit allows us to smooth our income and broaden investment opportunities. The ability can lead to better housing or further education and training.

Access to mortgages is an essential part of wealth procurement and can increase our status in society. When people are restricted from consumer loans, it can impair economic disadvantage and could increase poverty.

The norm for many years has been after graduating high school or college, you could depend on working and retiring from one job. Not anymore! In fact, the number of jobs people obtained during your lifetime will be somewhere between eight and eleven. The average ages were eighteen to forty-four; that's a new job for every 2.36 years! These findings show the necessity for a sold credit resume.

If you are currently unemployed and looking for a job or employed and looking to improve your economic reality, you've got a resume, right? Imagine for a second every bit of information contained in your resume was put there by someone else. Wouldn't you want to be sure what they were saying was 100% accurate and true?

You would want to know things like "was my name and address right documented properly?" or "are the correct dates of my employment listed?" The information could include something derogatory and cost you an employment opportunity. The mistake should upset you. The thought of

something like this happening should be alarming …
because it is every single day… on your credit report!

The credit scoring system in the US has a profound impact
on our daily lives. Your financial credit freedom is at risk.

The big three credit bureaus, employers, landlords and
insurance companies now use credit reports and scores to
make decisions that have a bearing on our social and
economic opportunities. These days, your credit history can
decide whether you get a job, an apartment, or access to
decent, affordable insurance and loans.

Is your credit score fair? This question stirs up controversy
every day. But it is an objective measure used to determine
if a loan made to a person today will be repaid on time. The
score is based on a person's credit history and other
objective factors that are demonstrably related to the
likelihood of default on future obligations. It is not affected
by an applicant's color, sex, race, religion, where they were
born, or where they live. If fair is taken to mean that
minority loan applicants are judged by the same objectives
with personal prejudice being no part of the equation, then
it is fair.

The US has a credit scoring system that is fair, but whether we like the consequences of its outcome may vary dramatically. Our financial resume is based on the decisions we made in the past. Hence, some observers argue that credit scoring may be unfair because it does not take into account special circumstances. The point is well taken, but I don't think the answer is to attack credit-scoring. The credit score is only one piece of information used by loan underwriters in determining whether a loan should be granted. Underwriters consider many factors, including special circumstances that may have affected the credit score. Indeed, as a larger part of their job has become automated, underwriters can and do pay increasing attention to special circumstances. Such flexibility has been encouraged by The Community Reinvestment Act, which presses depository institutions to meet the needs of low-and-moderate-income communities. Congress has also pressured the two large government-sponsored enterprises that buy mortgages in the secondary market, Fannie Mae and Freddie Mac, to do the same.

Yet, lender flexibility is not granted to loan money on an account that will become delinquent for sixty or ninety days every year. Rather, it means a willingness to work with you (or to refer you to others who will work with you) to set up a budget plan that will allow you to avoid delinquencies. There are many resources available to help you, but ultimately, the responsibility has to be yours.

Credit scores are nothing more than the output of a mathematical formula built to rank-order the likelihood that a person will repay the debts they have incurred. Credit scores were not built with racial bias, and minority statistics are not a written portion of the scoring process. The mathematical equation consists of numerical data only.

Finding Out Your Score

You can get a free copy of your credit report from Identity Guard, or a report from each of the three major reporting agencies–TransUnion, Experian, and Equifax–can be accessed once a year. So, stagger them four months apart, and you can stay on top of your credit all year long for free. But, these reports won't give you your score, just the background information agencies use to calculate the figures.

Chapter Two:
What is Credit?

Consumers apply for credit when they cannot afford to pay cash for various goods and services from their income or bank account. Credit is issued from a grantor whom you agree to repay in a timely fashion. The finance charges and time limit are decided at the point credit is granted.

Four Types of Credit

Revolving credit: Here consumers are given a maximum credit limit they can use to make purchases up to that limit. Each month, the balance or revolving debt is paid back with nominal payments. Most credit cards are a form of revolving credit.

Charge cards: When someone is issued a charge card, the process works in the same fashion as a revolving card but the balance must be paid in full every month.

Service credit: Consumer agreements with service providers are all credit arrangements. You receive electricity, cellular phone service, a gym membership, etc., (Four Types of Credit , 2018)

with the agreement that you will pay for them each month. Not all service accounts are reported in your credit history.

Installment credit: In this case, a creditor loans you a specific amount of money. The borrower agrees to repay the money and interest in regular installments of a fixed amount over a set period. Car loans and mortgages are two examples of installment credit.

Why Do You Need Credit?
The importance of good credit extends beyond just purchases, in that your credit information may be used by potential employers and landlords as part of the selection process. Good credit is necessary if you plan to make a major purchase such as a car or a home. Credit is a convenience that must be taken seriously, especially if you have an emergency.

Credit grantors review credit resumes and credit reports to determine financial risk. If they lend you money, extend credit, or give goods and services, will you pay them back? Your choices in life will affect your ability to gain credit. Some considerations on your financial resume are: residence tenor, employer statistics, balances in your bank account (and whether you have an account), savings account, and the length of service. The next focus is on what kind of assets you possess. The entire package determines whether you will be extended the credit.

What does good credit mean?

As mentioned previously, credit is more than just borrowing money. To a lender like an auto dealer or credit card company, credit is your reputation. Hence, your credit resume. This helps creditors see how likely you are to repay the funds and fulfill your obligation, and whether you will pay the agreed amount on time every month.

Good credit means you can be trusted to repay the borrowed money. The higher your trustworthiness means more opportunities. It increases the money that is available to you.

Take a car loan for example, a simple car loan. Say you have excellent credit and you take out a $10,000 loan to buy a new car. The interest rate could be 4.9% with a 60-month (5-year) payoff. This means you pay $188 each month, or $11,295 at the end of the five years. However, if you have no credit or bad credit and want to finance the same car, the results are very different. Because of your credit history, or lack thereof, you will end up paying additional costs overall. For example, if you receive an interest rate of 9.5% (or maybe even higher!), over 60 months you would pay $210 each month, or $12,601 in total. That's $1,300 more than if you had applied with good credit.

*The example above illustrates how credit history can affect you and should not be used as a guarantee for interest rates. *

The lesson is clear: Good credit saves you money! It is typically true whether you're looking at car loans, a home mortgage, credit cards, or any of the types of credit.

Also, many employers look at credit history to evaluate potential employees. Your credit history may indicate your ability to fulfill your agreements, background with finances, ability to handle multiple obligations or various other factors. While employers never use credit history as the only basis for hiring, it's becoming an increasing factor to compare or evaluate candidates.

In all, your credit history provides a glimpse of your character, your reliability, and your trustworthiness. Start building your financial reputation today.

Chapter Three:
Side Effects of Bad Credit

If you're maxing out your credit cards and ignoring your bills, it may not dawn on you how the miscalculation can affect your credit resume. Late credit card payments and the amount of debt you carry have the biggest impact on your credit score. Mess up in these areas and your credit score will plummet.

You might ask, "What's the big deal with a low credit score?" Many business judge people based on their credit resume. It's a simple way to get the best overview of a person's creditability history. The outcome may be loss of employment, difficulty finding a place to live, or an inability to gain utility services. Here are some of the most common side effects of bad credit.

1. **High interest rates on your credit cards and loans**

Credit scores indicate the likelihood that you will default on a credit card or loan obligation. Having a low credit score indicates you're a risk over someone with a better credit score. Creditors and lenders charge for this risk by increasing the interest rate you receive.

Bad credit borrowers pay substantially higher interest rates. The more you borrow, the more you'll pay in interest.

Credit and loan applications may not be approved

Creditors are willing to accept a certain amount of risk. However, low credit resumes will lead to an increased application denial.

2. Difficulty getting approved for an apartment

Many people don't realize landlords check credit before approving a rental application. Having bad credit can make it much more difficult to rent an apartment or house. If you find a landlord who will rent to you despite your low credit score, you may pay a higher security deposit.

3. How to rent with bad credit

Utility companies – electricity, phone, and cable – check your credit as part of the application process. If you have a bad credit history, you may have to pay a security deposit to establish service in your name, even if you've always paid your utility bills on time. The security deposit will be charged upfront before you can establish service in your name.

4.   You can't get a cell phone contract

Cell phone companies check your credit too. They argue that they're extending a month of service to you, so they need to know your reliability. If your credit's bad, you may have to get a prepaid cell phone, a month-to-month contract where phones are typically more expensive, or go without one.

If you're leasing or making payments on your cell phone, you may have to pay more upfront for a new phone or your payments may be higher if you have bad credit.

5.   You might get denied for employment

Certain jobs, especially those in upper management or the finance industry, require you to have a good credit history. You can be turned down for a job because of negative items on your credit report, especially high debt amounts, bankruptcy, or outstanding bills.

Note that employers check your credit report and not your credit score. They're not necessarily checking for bad credit, but for items that could affect your job performance.

6. Higher insurance premiums

Insurance companies check credit. They argue that lower credit scores are linked to more claims being filed. Because of this, they check your credit and charge a higher premium to those with lower credit scores, regardless of the number of claims you've filed.

7. Calls from debt collectors

Bad credit itself doesn't lead to debt collection calls. However, chances are that if you have bad credit you also have some past due bills that debt collectors are pursuing.

Difficulty starting your own business

Many new businesses need bank loans to help fund their startups. A bad credit history can limit the amount you're able to borrow, even if you have a solid business plan and data supporting your business success.

8. Difficulty purchasing a car

Banks check your credit before giving you a car loan. With bad credit, you might get denied a car loan altogether. Or, if you're approved, you'll likely have a high interest rate, which leads to a higher monthly payment, especially if you buy from a "no credit check" or a "buy here, pay here" car lot.

Regardless of how you got there, if you are dealing with poor credit, it's a good idea to make sure you understand the effects it can have on your financial freedom. Once you understand the effects, you'll want to know how to go about fixing your credit. Additionally, when you pull your own credit to check your score and report, this is considered a soft inquiry. When lenders or potential creditors pull your credit to evaluate your qualification for a loan or credit line, that's a hard inquiry. Only hard inquiries affect your score.

What is Debt Collection?

According to the Federal Trade Commission and the Consumer Financial Protection Bureau, debt collectors are one of the most complained about businesses, and with good reason. Few people have positive experiences dealing with debt collectors. Even the rare nice ones can be a nuisance simply due to the fact that they're calling for money. But it's typically cheaper for businesses to use collectors, so it's not likely that debt collectors are going anywhere anytime soon. (Federal Trade Commission , 2018)

A debt collection is a type of financial account that's been sent to a third-party debt collector. Debt collectors are companies who collect unpaid debts for others. The original company with which you created the debt most likely sent the account to the collection agency after you missed several payments and they were unable to get you to pay. It's usually more cost-effective for companies to hire debt collectors than to continue to spend their own resources pursuing payment on delinquent accounts.

Different creditors and lenders have different policies for sending accounts to collections. Reviewing your credit card or loan agreement will often give you some information about your creditor's timeline. Many credit card accounts are sent to a collection agency after 180 days, or six months, of non-payment. Other types of businesses may send accounts to collections agencies after just a month or two or missed payments.

What to expect when you have a collection account

When they're trying to get your debt paid, collectors will call you, send letters, and place the entry on your credit report. If they have your work phone number, they'll even call your place of employment, unless you let them know your employer doesn't approve. Some collectors have been known to show up at a person's home in their attempt to collect a debt. Surprisingly, that's legal. Debt collectors might even call your cell phone if you gave the number to your creditor to contact you.

Debt collectors can only call you between the hours of 8 a.m. and 9 p.m. your local time. They may call you several times a day, especially if you're dodging their phone calls. However, collectors are forbidden from calling you back-to-back in an attempt to annoy you.

When a debt collector has a hard time reaching you, they may call your friends or neighbors to make sure they have the correct contact information for you. They're allowed to do this, but they're not allowed to reveal that they're collecting a debt and they can't contact the same person more than once.

Debt collectors will send payment notices to the address they have on file for you. In their first bill to you, they have to notify you that you have 30 days to request validation for the debt. Requesting validation forces the debt collector to provide proof that you owe the debt. The debt validation notice may also be given to you over the phone if a phone call is the first time the collector is contacting you. If they don't have the correct address, you may never receive a notice of the debt. And if the collector doesn't have your correct phone number or address, you may not find out about the account until you see it listed on your credit report.

Debt collectors are required to follow the Fair Debt Collection Practices Act, or FDCPA, when they're collecting a debt from you. However, the thousands of complaints made against debt collectors each year proves they don't always follow the law.

How collections end up on your credit report

Your credit report contains information about your credit accounts, e.g. credit cards, loans, etc. Most, if not all, creditors send monthly updates about payment status to your credit report.

When an account is sent to a collection agency, either the original creditor or the collector updates the account on your credit report with a "collection" status. The creditor doesn't have to tell you that your account is being sent to collections. However, the debt collector does have to notify you that they are collecting the debt before they can take any action.

What does it mean for your credit?

A debt collection is one of the worst types of credit report accounts; it shows you have become seriously delinquent.

Your credit score will drop if a collection appears on your report. You may be denied for credit cards and loans in the future, especially if the collection is recent or remains unpaid, or both.

Debt collection accounts can stay on your credit report for up to seven years. You can lessen the effects of a collection on your credit score by paying the account, and as time passes, the collection will affect your credit less. Continuing to pay all your other bills on time will also help your credit score recover from a debt collection.

Debt Scams

Debt relief service scams target consumers with significant credit card debt by falsely promising to negotiate with their creditors to settle or otherwise reduce consumers' repayment obligations. These operations often charge cash-strapped consumers a large up-front fee, but then fail to help them settle or lower their debts – if they provide any service at all. Some debt relief scams even tout their services by using automated "robocalls" to consumers on the Do-Not-Call List. (Do Not Call List , n.d.)

Auto loan modification scams falsely promise that they can reduce consumers' monthly car loan or lease payments to help them avoid repossession. The FTC (Federal Trade Commission) also works to make sure consumers get a fair deal in the auto marketplace. (Federal Trade Commission , 2018)

Credit repair scams frequently target financially distressed consumers who are having credit problems. These operations lure consumers to purchase their services by falsely claiming they will remove negative information from consumers' credit reports even if that information is accurate.

The FTC has brought scores of law enforcement actions against these bogus credit-related services, and the agency has partnered with the states to bring hundreds of additional lawsuits. Further, in 2010, the FTC amended its Telemarketing Sales Rule to protect consumers seeking debt relief services like debt settlement or credit counseling. This rule prohibits for-profit companies that sell these services over the telephone. They cannot charge a fee before they actually settle or reduce a consumer's debt.

It also prohibits debt relief providers from making misrepresentations and requires that they disclose key information that consumers need in evaluating these services.

What is debt settlement?

It's a debt relief option that consists of contacting your creditors and settling your debt for much less than what you actually owe.

Why debt settlement works

When lenders such as credit card companies can't collect on your debt, they often decide to sell it to a debt collection agency. It is not unusual for them to sell it for twenty cents on the dollar or even ten cents on the dollar. This doesn't mean they will agree to settle your credit card debt for 20% or 10% of what you owe; however, in many cases; they will accept a decent offer – especially if you are having serious financial problems. In fact, the key to negotiating a good settlement is to convince your creditor that if they refuse to settle, your only recourse will be to declare bankruptcy.

The pros of debt settlement

The major pro or upside of debt settlement is that it is the only way to reduce your debt. It means you become debt-free in a much shorter time. The other techniques for managing debt include a consolidation loan, consumer credit counseling or credit card balance transfers. These can help you better manage your debts, but do nothing to reduce them.

Get rid of those persistent debt collectors

You can include all medical bills and unsecured debts in excess of $1,000 in your settlement arrangement. This should free you of those persistent debt collectors who keep calling and harassing you. Settled debts aren't subject to any legal actions or any other form of collection.

The cons or negatives of debt settlement

Before you start calling creditors and suggesting debt settlement, you shouldn't have made any payments on your debts for six months or more. This is bound to leave a black mark on your credit report and will definitely lower your credit score. Second, you may have to pay taxes on the debt that is forgiven. In other words, if you were able to settle $20,000 in debt for $10,000, you may have to pay income taxes on the $10,000 that was forgiven.

It is a gamble

Debt settlement can be a gamble because not all creditors will agree to settle. If you stop making payments on your debts for six months and then learn some of your creditors won't settle, you will be in even worse shape than when you started.

You will need to have cash in hand

The biggest con of debt settlement may be the fact that you must have the money available to pay your settlements. For example, if you were able to settle a $10,000 debt for $5,000, you have to have the $5,000 immediately. In fact, this is one of the selling points of debt settlement.

You can only settle unsecured loans

Debt settlement is a good solution for unsecured debts such as credit card debts, medical bills, personal loans or personal lines of credit. However, secured debts, including mortgages, homeowner's equity lines of credit and auto loans cannot be settled.

What is a charge-off?

Learning what charged off means and its impact on your credit report can help you make informed decisions to get your credit back on track. Here is what you need to know about the meaning of charged off.

Having a charged-off debt means you have not been paying the full minimum payment on money you borrowed for a significant amount of time. Because of the delinquent payments, your debt is re-categorized as "charged off" on the company's profit-and-loss statements. That means your creditor has accepted your delinquency.

The company considers the debt a loss and marks it charged off. They will either sell the debt to a collection agency or a debt buyer.

At that point, one debt may now appear twice on your credit report, compounding the confusion. One debt listing will be from the original company you borrowed money from, and the second listing is from the debt collector who purchased the account. Both debts will show up as active, which can make it frustrating to decipher.

Does a charge-off mean my debt is paid?

If your debt is charged off, that does not mean your account it cleared. Charged off is often used interchangeably with written off, sometimes leading people to believe the creditor has written off their balance and they no longer need to pay their debts. That is not the case. The company is writing off your debt as a loss for its own accounting purposes, but it still has the right to pursue collection of the past-due amount.

You are still legally obligated to pay back the money unless you settle (or file for certain types of bankruptcy) or the statute of limitations has been reached.

When will a charge-off happen?

Creditors will first try to send letters to remind you of a past-due bill. If that fails, they move on to a collections process. Re-categorization to "charged off" typically happens after your payment is 180 days past due, though installment loans (something along the lines of a mortgage, for example) can be charged off after 120 days of delinquency.

The six-month mark comes from a generally accepted accounting principle that determines 180 days to be the point after which receiving payment is highly unlikely.

It is important to note that debts can be charged off even if payments have been made, providing that all of the payments were below the account's monthly minimum.

Once the debt is charged off, the delinquency is reported to credit agencies.

How does a charge-off affect my credit report?

A charge-off is bad news for your credit report. Because a charge-off comes from missing payments, you will have late payments and a charge-off listed on your credit report. Negative information such as this leads to a lower credit score.

In fact, late and delinquent payments have the largest impact on your credit score: Up to 35% of your score is determined by your payment history. A lower credit score can cause everything from higher insurance rates to larger utility deposits to being denied credit.

How long does charged-off debt stay on my credit report?

Just like late payments, a charged-off account will remain on your credit report seven years from the date of the last scheduled payment before the account went delinquent. The time period does not start over again if the debt is sold to a collection agency or debt buyer. After the seven years, the charged-off account will automatically be removed from your credit report.

How to remove a charge-off from a credit report

To remove a charge-off from your credit report, you will first have to contact the original creditor to begin negotiations. You will have to convince the creditor that you need the charge-off removed, but in exchange you will provide payment of the debt owed. If you have a larger chunk of money available that you can use to pay on the debt, then you may have a better chance of succeeding at negotiating.

Before contacting the creditor, you should have a fairly good idea of how much you can realistically pay them on the account. It is also good to note that if the account is in collections, then there is nothing they can do to remove the charge-off (although they can remove the collection account). You must speak directly to the original creditor about possibly removing the charge-off.

You can also speak to the original creditor about a payment arrangement, however, make sure you do not provide them with any excuses or reasons as to why you weren't paying. All they want to know is if you are able to pay the debt you owe. Remain polite and professional while speaking to the creditor in charge of your charged off account.

What should I do if I have a charge-off?

The best thing to do is to pay the balance and settle the debt. Once paid, the report will show "paid charged-off." It won't remove the charge-off from your credit report, but it will show you are trying to resolve the negative account.

If you are unable to pay the debt in full, create a budget to find extra money to pay down the debt quicker. Paying your other debt on time each month is another great way to improve your credit report.

If you want to avoid having any of your accounts charged off, the best thing to do is take preventative measures. Learn and maintain positive financial habits and avoid living outside your means. Look into automating your finances as well to make sure you don't miss any payments on your cards and put yourself at risk for getting charged off.

Bottom line

When learning what a charge-off is and what you must do to get this negative mark on your credit report and settle your debt, you should take all the advice we have given and heed the suggestions while remembering the key points of a charge-off:

You are still responsible for paying off the debt even if the account has been charged off. This means the full amount owed to the original creditor, and they are able to attempt to collect the debt until the statute of limitations runs out.

You might end up making your payments to a third-party collection agency, or debt collector, rather than the original creditor depending on how much time has passed. If this is the case, however, be sure to practice extreme caution because there are many scams going around in regard to collection agencies.

Your credit will definitely suffer through the entire process because of bad debt. A charged off account is a big, bold black mark on your credit report and it will remain so even after the debt has been paid in full. However, it will look much better if your credit report says that you have paid the account or settled the charge-off, rather than sitting as unpaid with no positive notations.

Finally, if you are in debt and feel like you have nowhere to go, there are plenty of debt management programs to educate you on rebuilding your credit and digging yourself out of debt.

It is always better to avoid a charged off account in the first place. To do this, be sure that you are paying your accounts as agreed, and never allow your payments to become late or overdue. Increase your credit score by paying down credit balances so everything is in good standing.

Be sure you are checking credit reports from all three of the major credit bureaus because the information contained in each may differ.

Bankruptcy
Chapter 13

When most people think of bankruptcy, they imagine a situation where a court swoops in, takes all their assets, and leaves them with little or nothing. I'm happy to report that reality is much different. But that is the classic view of what we call a Chapter 7 straight bankruptcy case.

Chapter 7 is not the only type of bankruptcy available to us. There are five in all. You may have heard of Chapter 11, which companies often use to reorganize their debts. Ora Chapter 9, which is used by municipalities like a city or a public water utility to reorganize its debts under the protection of the bankruptcy court. Or even a Chapter 12, available only to farmers and fishing operations.

There is another type of bankruptcy that individuals use to reorganize their debts called Chapter 13 bankruptcy.

Unlike Chapter 7, it does not involve liquidation. Usually, a debtor (a person who files bankruptcy) is permitted to keep all of their property, whether it is exempt or not, as long as it complies with the law. Chapter 13 may also involve more expense than a Chapter 7 in terms of attorney's fees, as the process is more complicated and drawn out.

Time commitment

Chapter 7 is a comparatively brief process and usually only lasts four to six months before the court issues the discharge. On the other hand, Chapter 13 bankruptcy will last from three to five years, the length of a monthly payment plan you propose to the court to pay certain debts. The plan period will vary from three to five years, depending on whether your income is generally above or below the median income for your state of residence.

Payment plan

The Chapter 13 plan is simply a payment plan. It's an attempt to "reorganize" your debt over time. It's a great tool for the debtor who is behind in house or car payments. Those payments can be caught up with the payment plan over time, thereby saving the house from foreclosure or the car from repossession. The plan will also include any past due priority claims, like alimony, child support, or recent income taxes.

The Chapter 13 plan can also include payments to unsecured creditors like credit cards and medical bills. A calculation is applied to your income and expenses to determine if you have any disposable income after all your other obligations are met. You're expected to devote your disposable income to your payment plan, and that extra money will be used to pay unsecured creditors like those credit cards and medical bills. If you have no disposable income, that's okay; the debts will still be discharged because you've devoted your best effort to paying your bills.

Plan requirements

The Chapter 13 plan must meet several tests in order for it to be confirmed or approved by the bankruptcy court. First, the plan must be proposed in good faith. This means, essentially, that you intend to completely follow through on the plan and aren't attempting to misrepresent your finances or perpetrate a fraud on the court.

The proposal must meet the "best interest of creditors" test. In this section the test requires you to pay unsecured creditors at least what they would have received under a Chapter 7 bankruptcy.

In many cases, the unsecured creditors would have received nothing in Chapter 7, so this test can often be easily met. The other practice is called the "best efforts" test. It means you pay unsecured creditors a certain amount multiplied by the debtor's disposable income.

A trustee

Similar to the Chapter 7 trustee, the Chapter 13 trustee acts as the main point of contact for a debtor. The trustee will review the proposed payment plan and has the authority to challenge the plan in bankruptcy court if he or she believes it is improper. If the bankruptcy court confirms the proposal, the trustee acts as an intermediary between the debtor and creditors receiving payments. Specifically, the debtor makes payments each month to the trustee. The trustee then divides up the payment, as established in the Chapter 13 plan, and issues payments to the creditors.

Restrictions during chapter 13 bankruptcy

Chapter 13 carries a few more restrictions which are not present in Chapter 7 bankruptcy, the monthly payment plan being the most obvious. In addition, you will not be allowed to incur any more debt, like a car loan, without court approval. You must also maintain insurance on any collateral, like for a car loan.

Discharge

Similar to a Chapter 7 bankruptcy, at the end of the plan, most or all of your debts will be discharged. However, you may be left with debts that are not discharged, like student loans. As in Chapter 7, the discharge is personal, meaning if someone is obligated on one of the discharged debts, he or she is still liable for the debt.

Chapter 7

If you are having difficulty keeping up with your bills, and think how liberating it would feel to have a magic genie wish away your debt, it's not quite that simple. But, there are some federal laws that can help you manage or eliminate that obligation.

The single most common type of bankruptcy in the United States is Chapter 7. It is sometimes called straight bankruptcy. In a nutshell, the court appoints a trustee to oversee your case. Part of the trustee's job is to take your assets, sell them and distribute the money to the creditors who file proper claims. The trustee doesn't take all your property. You're allowed to keep enough "exempt" property to get a "fresh start."

Preparation

Before a case is filed, you'll have to gather all your financial records like bank statements, credit card statements, loan documents, and paystubs. You'll use that information to fill out the bankruptcy petition, schedules, statement of financial affairs, and other documents that will be filed with the court. You can download copies for free from the website maintained by the US Courts. Your attorney will use bankruptcy applications to produce them.

Broadly, these documents include the voluntary petition for relief, the schedules of assets and liabilities, declarations regarding debtor education, and the statement of financial affairs. These documents require you to open your financial life to the bankruptcy court. They include a listing of all of property, debts, creditors, income, expenses and property transfers, among other things. Once completed, you'll file with the clerk of your local bankruptcy court and pay a filing fee.

"If you're interested in finding your local court, visit the federal court locator page, choose "Bankruptcy" under "Court Type" and type your location in the bottom box."

Credit counseling

Almost every individual debtor who wants to file a Chapter 7 case has to participate in a session with an approved credit counselor before the case can be filed. This can be in person, online or over the telephone. The rationale behind this requirement is that some potential debtors don't know their options.

"A credit counselor may be able to suggest alternatives that will keep you out of bankruptcy. You can get more information about this requirement on the website for the U.S. Trustee."

Means test

A debtor must also successfully pass the means test calculation, which is another document that must be completed prior to filing for bankruptcy. This test, which was added to the Bankruptcy Code in 2005, calculates whether you are able to afford or have the "means" to pay at least a meaningful portion of your debts. The means test compares your income with the median income for your state. If you fail the means test, you can only file Chapter 7 bankruptcy under very specialized exceptions. Your alternative would be to file a Chapter 13 repayment plan case.

Meeting of creditors

After a Chapter 7 bankruptcy is filed, the court will issue a document giving notice to debtor's meeting of creditors. This notice is also sent to the creditors that are listed within the bankruptcy documents. During the meeting of creditors, the bankruptcy trustee will ask the debtor various questions about the bankruptcy, such as whether all of the information contained within the bankruptcy documents is true and correct. The trustee may ask other questions about a debtor's financial affairs.

If the trustee wishes to investigate the bankruptcy further, the meeting of creditors may be moved to a future date. It is important to note that at the meeting of creditors, as the name suggests, any creditor may appear and ask a debtor questions about their bankruptcy and finances. In reality, however, the only creditors who appear regularly are car creditors (to ask what you intend to do about your car payments) and the IRS (to ask when you're going to pay back those no dischargeable taxes).

Seizure of assets

If you have any non-exempt property, the bankruptcy trustee has the ability to seize and sell the property. Exemptions refer to federal or state statutes that allow you to protect certain types of property when you file bankruptcy. For example, exemptions exist to protect retirement accounts such as a 401(k) plan. Any assets that the trustee can recover are distributed to creditors.

Financial management course

Before most debtors can receive a discharge, they will have to take a course in financial management This class is likely taught by the same group that you used for the credit counseling. Plan to spend about one and a half hours in person, online or on the telephone.

Discharge

If the trustee and the creditors do not object to the debtor's discharge, the bankruptcy court will automatically give the debtor a discharge at some point after the last day to object. The last day to file a complaint objecting to a debtor's discharge is 60 days after the first session of the meeting of creditors. If no complaint is filed, the discharge is usually entered several days later. The discharge prevents creditors from attempting to collect any debt against you personally that arose prior to the filing of the bankruptcy.

Thus, for all intents and purposes, the discharge effectively wipes out debts. However, it is important to note that not all debts are dischargeable, including certain taxes and child or spousal support obligations. Furthermore, a discharge is personal. This means that a creditor can still collect on a discharged debt from a co-debtor that did not file for bankruptcy. A creditor with collateral may also be able to use that collateral to satisfy some of that outstanding debt.

What is liquidated debt?

Have you ever wondered whether you actually owe a creditor a certain amount of money? Have there ever been instances where you just weren't sure if you'd been charged, or whether your payment had been accepted, or even if you were responsible for a debt?

For many debts, it's not hard to figure out what you owe. Your creditor makes it easy for you by sending you a statement, usually monthly, setting out your charges, the interest that's accrued, any fees you've incurred, payments you made during the billing cycle, and your balance.

In certain situations, there are some accounts that have outstanding balances, and you may be unable to determine the amount that is owed.

These are called liquidated debts. When the balance owed is certain, an agreement can be determined by the borrower and lender in terms of a contract or possibly from a legal proceeding.

Unliquidated vs. Disputed or Contingent Debt

Closely related to the concept of liquidated debt is disputed and contingency debt.

A debt is disputed when some element of the contract or agreement between the parties is unclear. One party may deny that it has any responsibility for the debt at all. The borrower may dispute the balance because they haven't gotten credit for payments they have made.

A debt is contingent if some event must occur before the debtor becomes liable for the debt. A common example is a guarantor. The guarantor agrees to pay the debt, but only if the primary borrower defaults—doesn't pay or otherwise fails to meet the terms of the agreement.

A debt can be unliquidated, disputed, or contingent, and it could be two of those or all three.

Liquidated debts in bankruptcy

The status of a debt is important in the context of
a bankruptcy case. Debts have to be certain—or
liquidated—before a bankruptcy trustee can pay a claim.
Likewise, there must be no dispute or contingency
pending.

Examples of liquidated and unliquidated debt

Here are some examples of liquidated and unliquidated
debt. Debt can arise from many sources. For our purposes,
let's consider torts, which are civil wrongs that cause
damage to others or the property of others. We'll also look
at debt that arises from contract.

Liquidated tort debt

The Car Accident, Part 1: During rush hour one afternoon,
someone rear ended you, and you rear ended the car in
front. The driver ahead had to be taken to the hospital.
After treatment and getting an estimate on fixing his car,
the driver was out $4,379. He knows exactly how much
because he's got the bills and the estimate to prove it.
Unless you have some reason to dispute the amount, the
$4,379 is a liquidated debt.

The Car Accident, Part 2: Let's say that the driver suffered an injury that will require treatment for an extended period of time. Until that treatment is completed, the amount of the debt is unliquidated because no one knows exactly how much it will take to make the driver whole again, if at all. But, if you are found liable for the accident, you can come to an agreement to pay a certain sum to the driver and be released from any future responsibility for payments. Then the debt is liquidated because the parties have come to an agreement.

The Car Accident, Part 3: So, instead of coming to an agreement with the driver, let's say you dispute either how much you owe, or whether you're even liable for the accident (after all, someone rear ended you first.) The injured driver takes you to court and the judge or the jury finds that: 1. You caused the driver's injuries, and 2. You owe the driver $50,000. Because the court enters a judgment for a certain sum, the debt you owe is liquidated.

The situation can apply to similar situations. Your dog bites a neighbor. The neighbor sues you for defamation, lying about the bite on social media. You spray paint "dog hater" on your neighbor's fence. You get the picture.

Liquidated contractual debt

The Car Loan: Unliquidated debts aren't limited to accident situations; they can also occur when a contract is involved. For instance, you borrowed money to buy a car and you have a contract that requires you to pay $300 per month for 36 months for a total of $10,800. I would argue that the amount is liquidated. But after some time you acquire enough money pay off the loan early. The amount paid is $9,500. That, too, is a liquidated amount, because it's easily calculated. You and the lender both agree to the balance owed.

Consider what happens when you lose your job and can't make the payments anymore. The lender repossesses your car and puts it up for sale. If the lender doesn't get enough from the sale to pay off your debt, you'll be liable for the difference. But, until the car is sold, the debt is unliquidated. The final account balance cannot be determined.

It's possible, although highly unlikely, that the sale will bring in enough to pay the loan in full. So, the contingency is whether or not the sale pays off the loan.

Bankruptcy exemptions: Schedule C

Choosing your exemptions is critical to what property you keep after bankruptcy

One of the purposes of our bankruptcy system is to give people who have had financial issues a "fresh start." To that end, no bankruptcy is going to leave a debtor destitute. The debtor and his or her dependents will always be left with the basics for a new start. That will include furniture, clothing, household goods, even cars and equity in a homestead.

The property that you're allowed to keep in a bankruptcy case is called exempt property. So that the court and your creditors will know what property you intend to keep, the bankruptcy code requires that you affirmatively claim those exemptions.

Where do you find exemptions?

Bankruptcy exemptions are based in state and federal law, and each individual state has enacted its own exemptions. These exclusions apply to more than just bankruptcy cases; they also apply when a creditor obtains a judgment and wants to take property from the debtor to satisfy an account.

Congress has also passed a set of federal exemptions. Depending upon where you live and file for bankruptcy, the law of the state may permit you to only use the state exemptions, as opposed to the federal exemptions. For example, in California you may only choose state exemptions and not federal exemptions, but in Texas you can choose whether to apply the Texas state exemptions or the federal exemptions.

Consider getting professional help

Bankruptcy exemptions are complicated. Although you don't have to hire an attorney to represent you during the bankruptcy case, it very important to have assistance when you choose your exemption list. If you get it wrong, the consequences can range from uncomfortable to devastating.

Bankruptcy Schedule C

One of the documents you file with your bankruptcy paperwork is called Schedule C: The Property You Claim as Exempt, Official Form B 106C. Schedule C is arguably the most important document that you complete when filing for bankruptcy, no matter the chapter. Schedule C contains your claims of exemption. These exemptions permit you to keep property which would otherwise become property of the bankruptcy estate and the bankruptcy trustee.

Completing Schedule C

Part 1, Question 1

In Part 1 of Schedule C, you will notice that the document requires that you select a box if you are claiming exemptions pursuant to 11 U.S.C. section 522(b)(2) or 11 U.S.C. section 522(b)(3). If you choose state law exemptions, select 522(b)(3); section 522(b)(2) indicates that you have chosen federal law exemptions. Some states do not allow you to choose federal law exemptions. Consult with a bankruptcy lawyer to determine if this is the case in your state of residence.

Part 1, Question 2
Description of property
Starting with Question 2, you will list all of the property from Schedule A/B for which you claim an exemption. If you do not list property from Schedule A/B it will not be exempt, and the bankruptcy trustee may take it and sell it! You should use the same descriptions that you used in Schedule A/B.

Current value of the portion you own

You will also state the amount that is the current value of the portion of the property that you own. You can choose to list a specific amount. For example, in California, section 703.140(b)(3) allows residents to claim up to $550 per item. Thus, in that example, you would put $550 in the blank for the value. As an alternative, you can choose to say that you are claiming 100% of the fair market value, up to any limits listed in the applicable exemptions statute you are using.

Specific laws that allow exemptions

"In this section you will put the specific code section that provides for the exemption. For example, in California you would cite California Code of Civil Procedure section 703.140(b)(3) for exemptions in household goods and clothing. Each state has its own set of exemptions, and there are immunities contained in the bankruptcy code and in other federal statutes." For more, see Bankruptcy Exemptions by State

Part 1, Question 3

You will be asked if you are claiming an exemption in your homestead of more than a certain amount (which adjusts every three years), and whether you acquired the property more than 1,215 days before you filed the bankruptcy case. You are limited to a homestead exemption of a certain maximum amount if you obtained the homestead relatively recently. This is to prevent filers from converting non-exempt assets into cash and using that cash to purchase an expensive property not long before filing bankruptcy.

Part 2

The second page is just a continuation of Part 1, Question 2. You can also add additional pages as necessary to ensure that you have covered all property you wish to exempt.

Objections to your claims of exemption

After you file your bankruptcy, any creditor, the bankruptcy trustee, or the U.S. Trustee can object to your claims of exemption. This is done by filing a written objection with the bankruptcy court. A hearing will be conducted before a bankruptcy judge on the objection. A party may object to your claims of exemption for a variety of reasons, such as improperly categorized exemptions (claiming an exemption in clothes under an exemption statute for a car). An objection to your claims of exemption must be filed within 30 days after the trustee concludes your meeting of creditors, or within 30 days of any amendments to Schedule C.

Allowance of exemptions

If no one objects to your exemptions within the above-referenced 30-day period, your exemptions will be allowed by "operation of law." This means that your exemptions are automatically allowed and you don't have to be concerned that the trustee will come after any property that you've exempted. (United State Bankruptcy Court, 2018)

Chapter Four:
How is Your Credit Score Calculated?

How is your credit score calculated?

The traditional credit score is a three-digit number that calculates your reliability as a borrower. It can be used to predict whether you'll pay back your loans or pay debts on time, and determines if you are generally a good risk for lenders.

Credit scores typically range from 300 to 850. The three traditional credit reporting agencies (Equifax, Experian and TransUnion) calculate your score based on the information in the credit report.

The formula is based on several factors, including:

- ➢ Number of accounts
- ➢ Types of accounts
- ➢ Available credit
- ➢ Length of credit history
- ➢ Payment history

If the data in your credit report is inaccurate, it will hurt your score. It's important to generate a full credit report on a quarterly basis so you can identify any inaccuracies.

Additionally, any bankruptcies, collections, foreclosures or other financial defaults can negatively affect your credit score. Race, gender, marital status, nationality and religion are not factored into any credit-scoring models.

How Your FICO Credit Score is Calculated

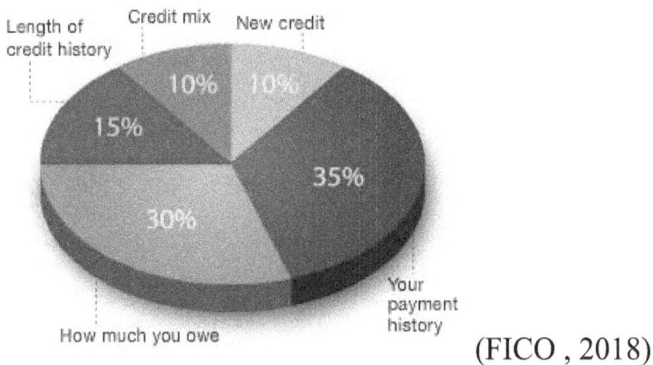

Length of credit history · Credit mix · New credit · Your payment history · How much you owe · 10% · 10% · 15% · 35% · 30%

(FICO , 2018)

Five common factors make up the calculated score.

Your credit score - a three-digit number used to determine how much money you can borrow and on what terms - is complex and enigmatic. But don't panic: The good news, it doesn't have to be a mystery.

Understanding the five components:

Payment history (or how you've handled credit in the past) equals 35 percent.

In the calculation of your credit score, no factor is more important than payment history. It's comprised of many complex components, but ultimately, experts say, it's pretty simple: Pay your bills on time, every payment schedule. Credit card and loan balances paid on time or early are the most important factor in your credit score.

Payment history is made up of several complex components, which can confuse borrowers. But, experts say that it basically boils down to never missing a payment, and your score will remain in good shape. If a problem occurs to force a late payment, contact the lender immediately and find a solution to the issue. Most lenders will work with you, as they understand situations occur that are out of your control.

The primary objective of a credit score is illustrate how likely you are to repay your debts. The higher your score, the more likely you are to qualify for a lower interest rate and a high credit limit. A high credit score can also help you qualify for the best insurance rates, car loans, home leases and mortgages.

- ➢ Credit utilization
- ➢ Credit length
- ➢ New credit
- ➢ Types of credit

Each amount is calculated differently, but payment history carries the most weigh with 35 percent of the score. Although, credit reporting agencies are secretive about many of the inner workings, their websites openly lay out the numerous components that make up a borrower's payment history. Those components include everything from information on loan accounts to delinquencies on any public records, such as bankruptcies and judgments.

Total debt Owed equals 30 percent If you want to earn a good score, you'll need to pay attention to your amounts owed – the second-most important factor used to calculate a borrower's score. This also includes the amount of debt incurred and the length of time carried.

How much money is owed to lenders is the second most important factor. It's nearly as important as paying your bills on time. But for some consumers, mastering their "amounts owed" can require a somewhat less-than-obvious approach.   Banks and other businesses use credit scores to predict the odds a borrower will repay a debt.

The score is calculated using five factors:

Payment history

➤ Debt vs. credit utilization ratio

➤ Length is credit history

➤ New credit accounts

➤ Types of credit

The "amounts owed" is used to calculate the number and types of accounts, along with how much debt is owed. Another key factor is the comparison between a borrower's available credit and the amount being used, or your credit utilization ratio.

Borrowers must be careful how much debt is carried if they hope to achieve a high credit score. The amount of debt carried tends to be predictive on their future credit performance. The amount a person owes has a direct impact on their ability to pay credit obligations.

There are six subcomponents of money owed:

➤ Amount of debt

➤ Number of debt accounts outstanding

➤ Amount of individual debt accounts

➤ Lack of debt types, in some cases.

➤ Percentage of revolving accounts, like credit cards.

➤ Percentage of debt owed on installment loans, like mortgages.

The debt credit limit compared to amount is crucial. It's the percentage of how much is owed compared to your credit limit amount. If you owe $100 on your credit card and have a $1,000 credit limit on it, your ratio is 10 percent.

Simple, right? Not always. Here's where it gets tricky: For example, FICO doesn't view all account types as being equal. Revolving balances (e.g., credit and retail cards) tend to carry more weight than installment debt (e.g., mortgages, auto and student loans) when amounts owed are considered. In the amounts owed category, credit cards are the most important type of account for achieving a high score, but they can also do more damage than other types of credit.

Additionally, while you might consider closing an unused or unwanted credit card to be a smart financial decision, because of the way your utilization ratio is calculated, FICO doesn't always see it that way.

As an example, imagine you have two credit cards, each with a $500 credit limit, for a total available credit of $1,000. One of the cards hasn't been used for a while and has a zero balance, while the other card has a balance of

$250. That gives you a utilization ratio of 25 percent - your $250 balance divided by your total $1,000 credit limit. You then close that unused card, eliminating the $500 credit limit associated with that account. Now, you've only got $500 in total credit available on that one card, but you still have $250 in debt. Suddenly, your credit utilization ratio has jumped to 50 percent.

The change can drag down your score despite your good intentions. But, you must do what is necessary to maintain your family's financial stability.

To improve the amount owed portion of your score, start by finding out how much credit you have available. Then, pay down balances. If you're a good customer, the banks may also grant requests to increase your revolving credit lines. Debt levels should remain less than 30 percent of account credit limits.

Another recommendation? Consider making payments to creditors more than once each month. Otherwise, if you put a major expense - like a new appliance - on a credit card, even if you plan to pay it off, your score may take a hit. The reason is credit scores are calculated as a snapshot in time, so if that happens to be right after you charged a new

$700 washing machine, your utilization ratio will look worryingly high. So, in this case making several smaller payments will help. In the end, it's a balancing act.

Length of credit history (or how long you've had credit) equals 15 percent.

It may not be the most important factor, but if you don't have a long credit history, you can probably forget ever having a perfect score. Plus, without at least some length of credit history, you won't have a score at all.

But, be cautious of taking on too much new credit all at once. It can hurt your credit score. However, adding some "new credit" to an old, troubled account may help your score by decreasing your credit utilization ratio.

The score is used to decide if you are a good credit risk. The score calculation is determined by several methods. To begin with, loan applications and new debts that were added in the last six to twelve months are considered. It isn't the biggest factor, but the appearance of "new credit" does influence a consumer's score. In FICO's view, it makes a borrower riskier, and thus will typically have a short-term damaging effect.

However, new credit can help your score by lowering your overall credit utilization. For example, let's say you own one credit card with a $5,000 limit and a balance of $4,000. Your credit utilization ratio is a whopping 80 percent – sure to be viewed as risky to potential lenders. However, if you're able to get a new card with a $10,000 limit and you don't use it right away, your credit utilization falls to a more palatable 27 percent.

New Credit makes up about 10 percent of a consumer's score, which ranges between 300 (poor credit) and 850 (excellent credit). New credit can help or hurt your score – it all depends on what else is in your credit history and how you plan to use the new accounts. In general, it's best to be conservative when applying for new credit. However, it doesn't mean you should be afraid to open a new account.

When you work to achieve a long history of responsible borrowing it will eventually lead to a high credit score. Recent studies have shown new loans or even applying for a loan can hurt your credit score short term. These borrowers are more likely to default on a loan or miss payments then those who have long term credit.

FICO considers the following factors:

➢ How many accounts have been opened in the past six to 12 months, as well as the proportion of accounts that are new, by account type?

➢ How many credit inquiries have been made recently?

➢ How long it's been since the opening of any new accounts, by account type.

➢ How long it's been since any credit inquiries. The re-appearance on a credit report of positive credit information for an account that had earlier payment problems.

The above list shows the first decline in a FICO score happens before a new account is even opened. When you apply for a loan, it results in what's called a "hard" credit inquiry, which happens when a bank checks your credit history to decide if it should approve the credit card or loan. (That's different from a "soft" inquiry, such as when you check your own credit report.) Only hard inquiries negatively impact a borrower's score.

Just how much damage does a hard inquiry do? For most people, it amounts to a loss of fewer than five points and inquiries fall off after two years. But it can vary.

Multiple credit inquiries over a short time frame – such as applying for five credit cards within a week – can multiply the score damage. However, with other types of new credit, FICO recognizes that borrowers typically shop around.

Therefore, the inquiries from multiple mortgage, auto and student loan applications won't hurt your score for 30 days, but all hard inquires will affect credit. Once a month has passed, the FICO scoring model treats multiple inquiries for one of those loan types as a single inquiry, provided the applications all took place within a relatively short window of time, such as 45 days. The consolidation helps limit the score damage that would otherwise be caused by multiple credit checks.

Other types of accounts that can hurt your score are certain new charge cards. The initial inquiry can lower the score, but once approved can lower the score once again.

Why that double penalty? Both items are predictive of future risk, as it indicates the consumer is seeking new credit. The same can also be said about the appearance of a new account without an inquiry on the credit report. The scoring formula is designed to assess risk by considering all information on the credit report, even if multiple pieces of information are pointing to the same action by the consumer.

To make things a little more complicated, in FICO's eyes, new credit isn't all bad. Recent "catch-up" payments for older delinquent accounts are treated as new credit and are positive for your score. The careful use of new loan accounts can help reduce the scoring impact from any past borrowing mistakes.

If a borrower brings past-due accounts current it's seen as a positive gesture under FICO's formula. Over time, as the months pass and the borrower makes additional on-time payments, the borrower's score will continue to heal from past mistakes.

However, since some older delinquent accounts may have already been closed, it's not always possible to get current on those troubled accounts. In those situations, FICO says simply adding new accounts – and always paying them on time – can help to rejuvenate the borrower's score, since they demonstrate the borrower is now acting more responsibly. Although, the initial hard inquiry may cause a score dip, a responsible borrower can expect to regain any lost points after a year.

If the new account is managed responsibly, you should see your credit scores come back once your credit history stabilizes.

FICO encourages borrowers to only open loan accounts they need. Credit counselors agree that taking on too many new accounts can cause problems. It's advised not to be reckless with applying for new credit cards. But, the fear of taking on new credit can be overblown. Besides, since new credit accounts only count for ten percent of a borrower's score, a careful application process can limit the scoring damage. Borrowers should focus on improving other aspects of their behavior rather than worrying about opening new accounts.

By understanding FICO's scoring model, borrowers can take the necessary steps to ensure they score well. Although credit reports typically include similar types of information, the data collected by each credit bureau can vary somewhat. The credit reports from the three major credit bureaus, for example, may include the following:

Installment loans, including auto loans, student loans and furniture purchases

- ➢ Mortgage loans
- ➢ Bank credit cards
- ➢ Retail credit cards
- ➢ Gas station credit cards
- ➢ Unpaid loans taken on by collection agencies or debt buyers
- ➢ Rental data

Some credit reports may include alternative data such as rent and utility bill payments. If you're tempted to go on a spending spree with your new plastic, adding another card to your wallet may not be wise. Focus on the fundamentals rather than applying for loans in an effort to boost your score, for most borrowers, it makes sense to focus on sensible credit spending.

A good score is more dependent on always paying bills on time, keeping credit card balances low and opening new loan accounts only when necessary. There is little reason for most borrowers to actively seek out a mix of credit.

Credit mix (or how many different types of loans you've taken out over the years) equals10 percent.

Want good credit? Responsible use of a single loan can get you there. But if you want a top credit score - the kind that gets you the best rates, the highest limits and the sweetest deals - you're going to have to mix it up a bit.

A variety of loans is necessary for maximizing your credit score. If you don't have several different types of loans, it won't kill your score. After all, the "types of credit" component is the least important of the five factors in the credit formula. But if you're striving for scoring perfection, the only way is to responsibly handle a good credit mix.

Lenders like to see consumers with a history of on-time payments across each type of account to demonstrate responsible credit management. It helps lenders understand a consumer's credit risk.

The idea of your credit regulation being used as a game might be unnerving, but it's true. While your credit score is a very serious matter, strategic management certainly starts to feel like a sport.

Consider the following: Many people are distressed to learn that even though they pay off their credit card balances in full each month, they're dinged on the amounts-owed portion of their score. Anytime you exceed a 30% credit utilization ratio during any billing cycle it can damage your credit score.

Don't stress; there are tactics you can use to get around this problem. In other words, you can win the credit utilization game. Here's how.

- ➤ Track how much you're charging to each card:
- ➤ Set up balance alerts
- ➤ Raise the credit limits on your cards
- ➤ Find out when your issuer reports to the credit bureaus
- ➤ Get in the habit of paying mid-cycle

> Track how much you're charging to each card

The easiest way to avoid losing points on your credit score is simply be aware of how much you charge to each card. Make a habit of patrolling your online accounts to watch your spending; if you start approaching 30% utilization on one card, make a payment or switch to using another card. Make it a rule to keep your balance below 30% on all your cards.

Your credit utilization is generally calculated on your total outstanding balances, compared with your total credit limit across all cards. But, some scoring models penalize you for exceeding 30% utilization on any one card. If you maintain your balance of 30% on cards you can beat the game.

Set up balance alerts

If you have a hard time remembering to check your accounts online, technology can help. Sign up with your issuer to receive balance alerts via text message or email. This way, you'll be sure to know when you're getting close to the dreaded 30% utilization threshold.

Pro tip: Set the alert to let you know when your balance reaches 20% of your available credit. That way, you have a little cushion of time to act before hitting set amount.

Raise the credit limits on your cards

If it's difficult to avoid utilizing more than 30% before the month is up, another solution might be to request a credit line increase on your card or cards. For example, if your credit limit is currently $5,000 but you usually charge $2,500 to your card every month, you're regularly hitting a 50% credit utilization ratio.

But if you raise your credit limit to $10,000, you can spend the same amount every month and only get as high as a 25% balance-to-limit ratio. This could make a big difference in your credit score.

Requesting a credit line increase might initiate a hard inquiry on your credit, but your score should bounce back quickly.

Find out when your issuer reports to the credit bureaus

In general, most credit card issuers report your balance and payment activity to the credit bureaus once a month. However, this doesn't necessarily coincide with your due date. If your issuer reports a few days before the end of your billing cycle, you'll consistently look like you're carrying a high balance - even if you pay it off in full just a few days later.

But this can be solved by placing a quick call to your card issuer's customer service line and asking when they report to the credit bureaus. Simply pay off as much of your balance as you can in advance of that date every month and you might see a jump in your score.

Chapter Five:

Hard and Soft Credit Inquires

Like most things in life, credit scores can be frustrating if you don't understand how they work. Did you know that:

There could be errors on your credit report that are damaging your score?

Not using your credit cards could backfire against you?

When some retailers and financial institutions access your credit report, the credit inquiries could hurt your score while other inquiries won't?

Not knowing these facts could seriously damage your creditworthiness in the eyes of potential lenders, so it's important to stay on top of your credit education.

Credit inquiries

> ➤ What exactly are they?
> ➤ Why are there different types, and more importantly, which ones can affect your credit?

What is a hard inquiry?

A hard inquiry is when a prospective lender checks your credit report to make a lending decision. Hard inquiries can lower your credit score slightly and will typically stay on your report for two years.

What is a soft inquiry?

A soft inquiry is an inquiry that occurs when a person or company checks your credit report as a background check, like when you check your credit score or a mortgage lender preapproves you for a loan. Soft inquiries can occur without your permission, but don't worry – they won't affect your credit in any way.

When do hard and soft inquiries occur?

Hard inquiries commonly take place when consumers apply for a credit card, auto loan, mortgage or other loan. On the other hand, soft inquiries typically occur when employers access your report to look for signs of risk or when you check your own credit report. Lenders may also use soft inquiries to preapprove you for a credit card or loan. Since they're not making a lending decision or guaranteeing approval – they're only saying you're likely to be approved for that credit card or loan – these inquiries are typically considered "promotional" and won't affect your score.

Unfortunately, there are some gray areas where either a hard or soft inquiry could occur, including when a bank needs to verify your identity or when you apply to rent an apartment or car. If you're worried about the growing number of hard inquiries on your report, ask the financial institution or company what kind of inquiry is necessary for the action to proceed. It will avoid unpleasant surprises.

Do inquiries affect my credit score?

While soft inquiries won't lower your score, hard inquiries could slightly lower your score. The good news is, hard inquiries typically don't affect your credit score by much – factors such as your payment history and credit utilization rate are usually weighted more heavily. However, the impact of an inquiry varies according to your credit history. If you have few accounts, a short credit history or a ton of inquiries, an additional hard inquiry could have a greater impact.

Keep in mind that when creditors see a lot of hard inquiries on a report, they become wary. Extending credit to someone with numerous hard inquiries looks like a consumer is desperate for credit, or was previously unable to get the credit needed from other lenders. In other words, a lot of inquiries may make you look like a higher-risk borrower, so it's best to minimize the enquiries.

Can I avoid hard inquiries?

If you want to apply for a new credit card or loan, there's no avoiding the subsequent hard inquiry. However, there is good news for those looking to shop around for the best deal on a mortgage or auto loan: Some credit scoring models will combine multiple inquiries within a certain period into just one. If you're going to rate shop, make sure you stay consistent and work fast. Credit bureaus usually pick up on the fact that you are comparison shopping and they will typically give a 14 to 45-day window to finish comparing.

In general, it's best to check your credit score and only apply for credit cards and loans for which you're most likely to qualify. This way, while you can't avoid credit inquiries, you can minimize the number of them. However, don't stress out about avoiding all hard inquiries. As mentioned before, while they do have the potential to damage your credit health, they generally play a minor role in your score.

How can I get rid of hard inquires I didn't approve?

If there's a hard inquiry on your report that you didn't authorize, simply call or write to the creditor, tell them you didn't authorize the inquiry and ask them to remove it. Alternatively, like any other incorrect information on your credit report, you can get rid of errors by disputing them directly with the credit bureaus. Your credit score is at stake, so you'll want to ensure the information is accurate.

The Bottom Line: Between the fear of being rejected and the possibility of your score dropping, applying for a new credit account can feel like a scary experience. But it doesn't need to be. Learn about which types of inquiries could affect your score, know how to avoid excessive inquiries and only apply for credit you'll likely be approved for, and you'll be able to get the credit needed.

Chapter Six:

Bank Accounts and Credit Scoring

Your credit score is more than just a three-digit number; it's an important financial tool that lenders use to determine how responsible you are when it comes to managing your money. There are several things that affect your credit score, including your payment history and amount of debt, but your banking habits can also make a difference. While swiping your debit card or writing a check won't affect your score directly, how you handle your bank account can impact your creditworthiness.

Do checking accounts affect your credit score?

Your traditional credit report only tracks your credit and debt situation. If you have a checking or savings account at a bank, credit union or brokerage firm, the following transactions will not appear on a credit report or credit score:

➢ Making a deposit or withdrawal

➢ Writing a check

> ➢ Closing an account
> ➢ Having multiple accounts

If you have a check overdraft, it still will not appear on your report unless you do not pay the fees and the bank turns the bill over to a collection agency.

There are a few instances where a checking account could affect your traditional credit score. Some banks or credit unions may look at your credit report when you open a new account. Usually they do a "soft pull," meaning they check your credit, but it does not affect your credit score. Some banks may do a "hard pull" or "hard inquiry," though usually those are only used by lenders when you request credit or a loan. If the bank does a hard pull, it will impact your credit score for up to 12 months, usually by dropping your score by five points or fewer.

The second way a checking account may affect your credit score is when signing up for overdraft protection on the account. It sets up a new line of credit, possibly triggering a credit report inquiry and a report from the bank to the three major credit reporting bureaus. But this is not always the case—not all overdraft accounts are reported. To find out if your account may be reported, ask your bank directly.

Even if a bank doesn't report a new checking account to the credit bureaus, it may check with ChexSystems, a consumer reporting agency for financial institutions. Banks report mishandled checking and savings accounts which in turn shares that information back to the banks and helps determine the risk of opening new accounts. Reports to ChexSystems stay on file for five years.

Opening new Accounts

When opening a new checking or savings account, the bank may decide to do a quick credit check before you're approved. The bank has the option of doing a hard or soft pull. A soft inquiry generally doesn't affect your score but a hard inquiry will show up on your credit history.

 If you're planning to open a new account, check with the bank first to see what kind of inquiry is required.

Closing an account

When it comes to your credit, the age of your accounts is a major factor in determining your score. The longer a credit card or line of credit has been open, the better. Therefore, closing older credit card accounts can work against you. When you close a checking account, age isn't a factor but it's still possible that it could affect your score.

If you're closing an account with an outstanding overdraft or the bank closes your account because it suspects fraud or other criminal activity, it could show up on your credit. Whether the information is reported through ChexSystems or the three major credit reporting bureaus is ultimately up to the bank. If, however, you're closing an account because you've found a better deal somewhere else, your bank can't hold this against you.

Banks are responsible for reporting negative information to ChexSystems. Some of the reasons you may be reported include frequent bounced checks, excessive overdraft fees or abandoning an account with a negative balance. If you write a check to a business that uses ChexSystems, the transaction may be denied based on the information in your file.

Overdrafts and your credit score

Overdraft simply means that you've spent more money than you had in your account. Typically, the bank covers the difference and charges you a fee for doing so. Overdrafts can occur for several reasons. Maybe you wrote a check and forgot about it or a deposit didn't clear right away. When it only happens once, an overdraft usually isn't that big of a deal.

If, however, you've racked up a significant amount of overdraft and you don't have enough cash to bring your account out of the red it can mean trouble where your credit's concerned. Eventually, the bank may decide to close your account and refer the debt to a collection agency. At this point, you'll likely receive a black mark on your credit that can stay in place for up to seven years.

Virtually all banks now offer some form of overdraft protection, although you may have to specifically request this service. Depending on the bank, you may be charged a separate service fee if you decide to opt-in. Certain banks offer overdraft protection that's reported as a revolving account or line of credit. Credit reporting bureaus view this the same as a credit card when calculating your score. If you routinely keep a low balance in your checking account, signing up for overdraft protection a wise decision.

Bouncing checks

It used to be that if you wrote a check, it would take a week or more to clear. Nowadays, checks can clear in a matter of one or two days, which makes it vital that you have enough money in your account. To cut down on the number of bad checks they receive, many businesses choose to use

ChexSystems, which is a check verification and credit reporting agency.

Chapter Seven:

Debt vs Income Ratio

Debt-to-income ratio

We all understand the concept of incoming funds and outgoing bills. The multiple recurring bills, everything from cell phone to internet, not including mortgage or rent. Plus, you can add gas expenses, groceries, and credit card debt. Sound familiar?

Some months you feel like all your money goes out to pay debts instead of adding to your retirement fund or other savings. This could mean you have a high debt-to-income ratio (DTI) situation. The debt-to-income ratio is a number that expresses the relationship between your total monthly debt and your gross monthly income. Here's the formula:

DTI = total monthly debt payments/gross monthly income

Say you pay $1,600 a month on your mortgage. You pay $400 a month for your student loans and have no other debt. Your total monthly debt payments come to $2,000.

Your gross monthly income is the money you earn before taxes and deductions. If that's $6,000, your DTI is 33%.

Why the debt-to-income ratio is important

From your perspective, the debt-to-income ratio is an important number to watch. The amounts generate the stability of your financial situation. If your debt is 60% of your income, any hit will leave you scrambling. If you must step up your spending in other areas (medical expenses, for example), you'll have a harder time keeping up with your debt payments than someone with a DTI of 25%.

From the perspective of creditors and lenders, the DTI is an important measure of risk. Folks with higher debt-to-income ratios are more likely to default on their mortgages and other debt. When you apply for a mortgage, calculating your DTI will be part of the mortgage underwriting process. In general, 43% is the highest DTI you can have and still get a Qualified Mortgage. And you want a Qualified Mortgage because it comes with more borrower protections, such as limits on fees.

What's a good debt-to-income ratio?

If 43% is the maximum debt-to-income ratio you can have while still meeting the requirements for a Qualified

Mortgage, what counts as a good debt-to-income ratio? Generally, the answer is a ratio at or below 36%. The 36% Rule states that your DTI should never pass 36%. A DTI of 36% gives you more wiggle room than a DTI of 43%, leaving you less vulnerable to changes in your income and expenses. Of course, if you can manage your finances in such a way that your DTI is, say, 18%, so much the better.

The debt-to-income ratio is an important measure of your financial security. The lower it is, the more affordable your debts. With a low DTI, you can likely weather storms better and take risks. If you want to take a job that pays less but is in a field you've always dreamed about joining, you won't have to worry as much about adjusting to a lower income. Plus, debt = stress. The higher your DTI, the more you can start to feel like you're on a treadmill, working just to pay off your creditors. No one wants that.

Chapter Eight:

Dealing with Negative Credit Issues

The idea of having lingering debts can be exhausting. It puts a stress on your income and peace of mind. But before you can become debt-free, you need to find out how much you really owe. The only way to accomplish this task is to check your credit report from a reputable business. Then, once you review your report and determine what accounts are delinquent you can begin to list the collection agencies. Although paying off the accounts in collections might not improve your credit score, it will show lenders that you've made good on your past debts. In fact, some lenders require that you take care of all delinquent debts before they approve you for a new loan.

What is Collections?

When a borrower fails to pay a debt on time, the creditor can turn it over to a debt collection agency, thereby putting the debt into "collections." Typically, your creditor will try to collect from you for three to six months, and some are willing to work out a deal to pay off your debt. If you don't pay, however, your creditor might opt to work with a debt collector.

Your creditor can either assign a debt collector to collect the debt — and pay the collector a fraction of the proceeds — or simply sell the debt outright. In the latter case, the debt collector gets to keep whatever money is recovered.

How can I learn if I have debt in collections?

To find out if you have debt in collections, take these steps:

Check Your Credit Report

The first step is checking your credit report. You can obtain a free credit report from each of the three major credit bureaus — Equifax, Experian and TransUnion — once every 12 months from AnnualCreditReport.com. If you have any accounts in collections, they'll show up as separate records on your report.

Find out if a credit agency tried to contact you

Debt collection agencies only get paid if they collect from you, so usually you'll know if you have accounts in collections. However, if you've moved or changed your phone number, a collection agency could be trying to reach you at an old number. If you see a collection account on your credit score, contact the creditor listed.

Ask the original creditors

If you know you have an old debt that you haven't paid but aren't sure whom you owe now, contact the original creditor. The creditor should be able to tell you if the debt was assigned or sold to a collection agency. If the debt has been sold, however, the original creditor might not be able to negotiate with you even if they want to.

Get contact info from your credit report

You can learn how to pay collections by checking your credit report. Your report should contain all the information necessary for you to get in touch with a debt collection company. Collections appearing on your credit report will hurt your credit score, but calling collection agencies for information won't even appear on your report.

What should I do if I have debt in collections?

Pay the Debt in Full

The most straightforward way to deal with debt in collections is to pay off what you owe. Make sure, however, that you're paying the right party. If your debt has been sold, you can't just pay the original creditor, because the collection agency owns the debt. But remember that paying off your debt might not affect your credit score. Your credit report will be updated to show that the collection account has been paid off, but the information will remain on your report for seven years after the original delinquency date.

Negotiate the debt

If you can't pay back the debt in its entirety, you might be able to negotiate by paying back a smaller amount in exchange for the creditor forgiving what remains. First, make sure you're negotiating with the entity that owns your debt, whether that's the collection agency or the original creditor.

When negotiating, you can offer to make a lump sum payment or create a new payment plan with more flexibility. But, remember that the creditor doesn't have to make a deal. If you do reach an agreement, make sure you get it in writing so you have proof of the terms if the creditor ever comes back and says you still owe money.

Dispute the debt

In some cases, the debt might legitimately not be yours, such as if you've had your identity stolen. If you receive a notice from a collection agency for a debt that isn't yours, dispute it in writing within 30 days. Once the collection agency receives your dispute, it must cease contacting you until it has provided verification of the debt. You should also dispute the information with each of the credit bureaus and provide as much information as possible to show that you didn't take out the original debt.

Know your rights

A collection agency must provide you with the following information within five days of contacting you:

> ➤ The creditor's name
> ➤ The amount you owe

You have a right to dispute the debt within 30 days. If you don't appeal the collector will assume the debt is valid.

Debt collectors are prohibited from deceiving you when trying to collect a debt. For example, the debt collector can't say you've committed a crime when you haven't, falsely claim to work for the government, threaten to garnish your paycheck if they aren't legally able to do so, or make other false threats. If you receive a call with some threats it may be a scam, so do not give them any information. Request contact by mail or email. Get the information in writing before you proceed.

How do debt collection agencies work?

Debt collection agencies make money by collecting delinquent debts. Sometimes, the debt collection agency acts on behalf of your original creditor and gets paid a portion of what's recovered. In other cases, it will purchase the debt from the original creditor for a fraction of the actual value. The collector will keep all the recovered debt.

How much does a collection agency pay for a debt?

The amounts collection agencies pay for debts vary, but it can be as little as pennies on the dollar. When you're talking to collection agencies, beware that you could be asked to pay a debt that is past the statute of limitations. Consumers can sue collectors who try to collect a debt that's no longer within the statute of limitations.

Can a debt collection agency take you to court?

Yes, a debt collection agency can take you to court. If the court finds the debt is legally enforceable, the debt collection agency could garnish a portion of your wages, seize bank accounts or record liens against your real property, such as your house. This allows creditors to get paid if your home is sold or refinanced.

Does your old debt have an expiration date?

If you have some negative debt reflected on your credit reports, you may be wondering how long debt collectors can try to collect on that debt, and how long that debt can affect your credit. The simple answer is, it depends. The full answer requires some explanation…so let's start with collections.

How long can old debts be collected?

Each state has a law referred to as a "statute of limitations," which spells out the time during which creditors or collectors may sue borrowers to collect debts. In most states, they run between 4-6 years after the last payment was made on the debt.

A debt that is outside the statute of limitations is called a "time-barred" debt.

In some states, collectors cannot try to collect at all once a debt is past the statute of limitations. In other states, they cannot sue you but they may still try to collect the debt.

Does that mean that once the statute of limitations has expired you won't be sued for a debt? Not necessarily. Some debt buyers — companies that buy and try to collect very old debts — still go after borrowers and even take them to court. They know that most borrowers who are sued for old debts won't show up in court and the judge will issue a "default judgement," which may give them additional collection powers such as access to the money a debtor has in his or her bank account, or the ability to garnish wages to collect the judgment. To prevent this, all a borrower must do is appear in court at the appointed time and explain that the debt is time barred. If that is correct, the lawsuit will be dismissed.

If you are contacted by a collection agency about a very old debt:

Ask the debt collector to send you written notice of the debt. This is required under the federal Fair Debt Collection Practices Act, (Federal Trade Commission, n.d.) even if you don't ask. But by keeping the initial phone conversation to a minimum, you may avoid saying or doing something that could hurt you later. (Scammers will say they aren't allowed or will offer to email you something. Don't accept that answer.)

Once you receive written notice of the debt, you have 30 days to request validation of the debt. Mail your request to the collector with a certified letter and simply ask them to validate the debt. You don't have to give a reason for your request. You can simply say, I dispute this debt, please validate it.

While you are waiting for the response from the bill collector, contact a consumer law attorney or your state attorney general's office to confirm the statute of limitations for the debt. (Consumer law attorneys who regularly represent consumers in cases against debt collectors often provide a free consultation.)

If you confirm the debt is too old, you have one of three choices. You can:

Pay the debt

If you know you owe the debt and you can pay it, you can do so. Make sure you keep written records of the amount due and your payment. Sometimes these old debts get sold to multiple collection agencies and if you get another call about this debt you want to have proof that you have paid it.

Settle the debt

If you know you owe the debt and want to try to make good, but you can't pay the full amount (or if the debt has been inflated by fees), then you may want to negotiate to settle it for less than the full amount due. This is tricky, though, because once you start negotiating you could reset the statute of limitations, and might wind up being sued for the entire debt. If you really want to go this route, your best bet is to talk with an attorney.

Send the collector a letter telling them to leave you alone. You have the right to ask a debt collector to stop contacting you. Once you do that, they are only allowed to contact you to tell you if they are taking legal action against you. If you know the debt is outside the statute of limitations, state that in your letter and tell them not to contact you again. Don't be surprised if they sell the debt to someone else, but they shouldn't bother you again.

How long do collections affect my credit?

Don't confuse the statute of limitations with the amount of time that collection accounts can appear on credit reports. They are two separate issues.

The length of time that collection accounts may remain on credit reports is seven years and 180 days from the date the consumer first falls behind on the original account. This requirement is found in the Fair Credit Reporting Act, a federal law.

The CRTP (Credit Reporting Time Period) for collections is up to 7.5 years from the DoFD (Date of First Delinquency) on the OC (Original Creditor) account that led to the collection. The DoFD is the first date that someone gets behind on payments and never again gets caught up.

Even if one of these bills remains unpaid, it cannot be reported after that 7.5 years is completed. The date an account was placed for collections is irrelevant here, so don't let that confuse you.

The only scenario where an old collection account can affect your credit is if you are sued and the collector gets a judgment against you. That new judgment would have its own 7-year reporting period. You can get your free annual credit reports to see if you're facing a judgment. You can also see the impact that judgment is having on your credit scores for free on Credit.com.

If you have a debt collector trying to collect a debt from you that you think is too old for them to legally collect, it's important to find out the statute of limitations in your state. If it turns out the debt is not time-barred, then paying or settling it may protect you from being sued. But if it is too old, then you can choose to either pay it or send the collection agency a cease contact letter.

How the credit scoring models view paid collections?

The newest FICO score model 9 treats collections differently than previous FICO models in that it will ignore paid collections in the score calculation (and unpaid medical collections will have less of an impact on score than previous models). Vantage Score 3.0 also ignores collections with a zero balance. So, the good news is that paying off a collection account will raise your credit score with these two new scoring models. The bad news is that most lenders and creditors are not using these new score models, with older FICO models currently in place, even though VantageScore use continues to grow.

One thing to remember with paid collections is that the further in the past it becomes, the more your score will rise going forward, little by little, if all positive credit factors such as on-time payments and low debt usage are followed.

Even though the newest credit scoring models may ignore paid collections, these accounts still appear in your credit file with the three major credit bureaus. *Or do they?*

How the collections agencies view paid collections

The whole purpose of collections agencies reporting an unpaid debt to the credit bureau is to encourage you to pay your debt or suffer this harmful blemish to your credit report. But once a debt is already reported to the credit bureau, there's not much incentive for you to pay.

For collections agencies, they've accomplished their goal if they've gotten you to pay the debt in full or even on an agreement that the debt is satisfied for less than the full balance. Together with the newest credit scoring models, some collections agencies don't see the need for continuing to report a debt that was paid. In fact, to stop reporting on it or have it removed from your credit report entirely might be an incentive for you to pay. In accordance with the Fair Credit Reporting Act, these creditors are obligated to report accounts accurately, which says nothing about not reporting the accounts at all.

Most collections accounts, even when paid, will stay on your credit report for the full 7 years, with a status marked "paid." The only time a creditor or collections agency is obligated to stop reporting your collections account and have it deleted from your credit reports is if there was an error in the reporting of the debt. You can dispute errors on your credit reports to have them removed. Beware, though, that if the error was minor and clerical and you really do owe the debt, it can show up again the following month, this time reported accurately. If you still owe the debt, the collections agencies are required to report it.

But some collections agencies have recently been more amenable to advising the credit bureau to delete your collections account entirely after they receive a full payment on a debt or you make an agreement with them to satisfy the debt for less than the full balance owed. Some say they will not report debts at all if satisfied within a specified short time period.

Some of their threats have no teeth

If you can't pay the collector the amount they are demanding or refuse to give your bank account or debit card number to make the payment, the debt collector may threaten to "put you down for 'refusal to pay'." But that's "a meaningless phrase in the debt collection world."

When a collector says, "We are going to inform your creditor that you are refusing to pay this bill!" they are just using reverse psychology. Your creditor has already figured out that you aren't paying the bill, or they would not have sent your account to a collection agency in the first place!

Another example: Collectors will always try to create a false sense of urgency by imposing a series of deadlines, after which "this deal will no longer be available." The reality is that settlement or workout offers tend to improve over the course of a typical 3-month collection assignment (i.e., in a non-legal collection scenario).

They must stop bugging you at work if you tell them. The Fair Debt Collection Practices Act is very clear on this point. Once you tell a debt collector your employer doesn't allow you to talk while you are at work, they must stop calling your place of employment.

They can't discuss your debts with anyone else

Debt collectors are generally only allowed to discuss your debt with you, a cosigner, your spouse, or your attorney. They cannot discuss your debt with neighbors, relatives who aren't obligated to pay the debt, or coworkers.

What is a public record?

Public records are information pertaining to legal matters that have a direct impact on your finances. They list things like paid and unpaid debts, legal liabilities, and your payment history.

They tell a creditor if you are a good risk for a loan. When you are taken to small claims court and a judge makes a ruling against you, this judgment is considered a public record.

Foreclosures, bankruptcy, liens, judgments, and lawsuits are all public records that the government is required to file and keep available for the public. Most records stay on your credit report for 7 years; however, some may remain up to 10 years.

What kind of information is included in a public record?

If you file for bankruptcy, the amount the court found you legally responsible to pay will be listed, plus an exempt amount that the court says you are not responsible to pay.

Lastly, there will be an asset amount for the number of personal assets the court used to make its decision. These will all be listed under the bankruptcy and are the kind of public records that can significantly lower your credit rating and affect your borrowing power.

Some other items you might find in a public record are financial counseling, a financial statement, garnishments, and financial marital claims from a divorce. However, all these things affect your income and thus affect your credit.

What information is not part of your public record?

You may feel like your whole life is on display, but that's not entirely true. There are a few categories of strictly confidential records which are protected by law. Confidential records include welfare benefits, income tax, your education level, and medical and criminal records.

These records are kept confidential because they contain Social Security numbers, your contact information, health history and your financial information.

How are public records made public?

The government takes making public records available to the public very seriously. It runs a service called PACER that is provided by the federal judiciary. PACER is short for Public Access to Court Electronic Records.

PACER is an electronic public access service, and it lets users get case and docket information from federal appellate, district, and bankruptcy courts via the Internet.

The federal website for PACER says that it currently hosts over 500 million case file documents. These are available immediately after they have been electronically filed.

However, this is only one of the ways your records become public. It also allows your information to be reported to the three credit reporting agencies.

Do public records affect your credit score?

Public records on your credit report have an impact on your credit score. They can be a deciding factor when a lender is making a financial decision.

The process of removing the blemishes can be a time-consuming or frustrating job but imperative you have these items removed. You may choose to hire a professional, remember your time is important. It is always better if the public records portion of your credit report is empty.

The effects of late payments

Lenders consider payment history when evaluating your credit risk and deciding whether to approve you for credit. A long-standing history of on-time payments suggests that you are a responsible and reliable borrower; a poor history of on-time payments suggests that you may not repay debts and could result in a costly loss to the lender.

Being unreliable with payments is a red flag to financial institutions, and several things can occur when you pay late.

You'll usually be charged a late fee. If you pay your credit card bill a single day after the due date, you could be charged a late fee of $25 to $35, which will be reflected on your next billing statement. If you continue to miss the due date, you can incur additional late fees.

Your interest rates may rise. Paying your creditors late may result in an increase in your interest rate, often resetting your interest rate to a penalty (or default) APR. For credit cards, the penalty APR is often as high as 29.99 percent, which means you'll pay significantly more in interest on your outstanding balance if it's triggered. If you have a promotional 0 percent APR on a balance transfer credit card, paying late may also forfeit your 0 percent promotional rate and reset it to the default interest rate.

It may end up on your credit report. If your payment is more than 30 days late, the three major credit bureaus are usually notified, meaning the late payment will show up on your credit report. A late payment on your credit report could stay there for seven years.

It might decrease your credit score. Payment history information typically accounts for nearly 35 percent of your credit score, making it one of the single most important factors in calculating your score. Just one late payment can drastically lower your credit score, especially if you have a good or excellent credit score. Depending on how late your payment is, how frequently you pay late and what your credit score is, late payments can severely affect your credit.

Paying late is a dangerous credit habit that could lead to more damaging credit actions, such as neglecting an account until it becomes delinquent or sent to collections. An account in collections may remain on your credit report for seven years and cause even more damage than a late payment.

What to do if you've made a late payment

If your bills are past due, the sooner you can pay the bill, the better. The damaging effect of a late payment on your credit score can increase the longer the delinquency.

If you've made a late payment recently, you could attempt to do the following:

Request removal of a late payment fee. If you're in otherwise good standing with your bank, consider getting in touch with them and requesting that the late fee be forgiven and removed.

Work to reset your penalty interest rate. If a late payment caused your interest rate to increase, your issuer is generally required to reset your interest rate back to the pre-penalty rate if you make six months of on-time payments, so get back on track and start making on-time payments.

Pay all accounts on time. If a late payment caused your credit score to drop, the best thing you can do is to continue on-time payments on all your accounts. After a few months of consistent on-time payments, your credit score could slowly improve. An easy way to prevent late payments is to set up automatic payments and email or text reminders on your financial accounts.

Finally, keep track of your overall credit health by checking your free credit reports on Credit Karma. They break down the factors that can affect your score, so you can keep an eye on your payment history as well as other important areas. Paying on time every month could help you build good credit history and improve your credit score over time.

Chapter Nine:
Credit Report in Minority Environments

Whether we want to admit reality, our credit score carries tremendous weight in society. A high credit score makes it easier to get loans for important life events like buying your first home, getting a new car, or even starting your own small business. However, data from the FBI has shown that minorities tend to have much lower credit scores than their majority counterparts, making it harder for nonwhite Americans to gain access to the financial institutions and resources that are necessary to get ahead in modern life. For this reason, some might argue that credit scores are racist.

Are credit scores racist? Can a credit bureau discriminate based on race when it comes to assigned credit scores? Let's find out.

How credit reports reflect racial disparities

It's against the law for credit bureaus to take someone's race into account when preparing their credit report.

Likewise, the Equal Credit Opportunity Act prevents lenders from denying a loan or charging unfair interest rates based on a borrower's race.

However, this does not mean that credit scores don't reflect deep economic divisions among people of different races and backgrounds. A poll found that 62 percent of indebted white households have "excellent" or "good" credit scores. Compare this with 44 percent of African-American households that also carried debt.

While the law prevents credit bureaus from using race to determine credit score, there are some factors that are correlated with race and that indirectly affect a person's credit score. Among these are:

Income — How much money you make goes a long way towards determining your credit score. Having a higher income gives you more power to pay off any loans and pay off your credit card balance each month.
Historically, minorities have been (and continue to be) underpaid in the United States, leading to sharp differences in income between white and nonwhite Americans.

Family credit history — Although parents can't directly influence their children's credit scores with their own credit history, having a strong credit history that runs in the family can improve a person's credit score. Parents who have good credit of their own are more likely to teach good credit habits to their children. Parents who had their children as authorized users can also give their kids real-world experience with credit before they leave the nest. Decades of financial discrimination against minorities have made it hard for these families to build good credit habits over the generations.

Location — Location is correlated with credit score, so poor neighborhoods often have much lower credit scores than their wealthy counterparts. Since minority populations are often grouped together in low income neighborhoods, these areas have lower credit scores on average.

Although race cannot be factored directly into a person's credit score, the credit differences that exist across racial lines reflect deep economic divisions between people of different races and their histories of working and living in America.

How credit scoring reinforces racial inequality

Not only do credit scores reflect racial inequalities when it comes to financial power, they also reinforce those very same divisions. Here's how credit scores perpetuate these racial divisions.

A low credit score makes it harder to take out personal loans. Personal loans play a big part in today's economy, where big purchases like a new home or car are impossible for almost anyone to make with the cash in their bank account.

When it comes to private student loans, having parents with a good credit score can be crucial. Since many students haven't yet developed their credit history, private lenders will want the reassurance of having a parent cosign. However, if your parents don't have a good credit score, you won't be able to get as good a deal on private student loans.

Starting a small business usually requires loans, since no one person has the money to cover the costs of opening and operating a business. However, before your business credit score is established, lenders will want to look at your personal credit score. This can make it harder for minorities to start their own businesses, even if that business would help them get ahead economically.

Predatory lenders tend congregate in neighborhoods with a high minority population. These lenders will take advantage of an area's need for emergency cash by offering things like payday loans and car title loans. These loans will come with unreasonably high interest rates and fees, making it impossible for borrowers to pay them off. Becoming the victim of predatory lenders will just cause a person's credit score to go down even further.

Credit bureaus are prohibited from discriminating based on race, but that doesn't mean that credit scores aren't racist. Today, credit scores reflect racial differences in economic status. Even more, though, they contribute to deepening those divisions by making it harder for minorities to access the financial resources necessary to improve their economic standing, and by attracting predatory lenders who just make the situation worse.

Chapter Ten:
Fixing Your Credit

Credit report mistakes can lead to disqualification for mortgages and car loans, as well as increased insurance premiums and interest rates. In some cases, those mistakes can even prevent you from getting a job.

Some consumers have started enlisting law firms to dispute negative items on their credit reports...and they've been wildly successful! But, it's not necessary. The DIY approach is available. 79% of consumers who disputed credit report errors were successful in removing them.

Are you wondering what you can do to fix your credit score, or if it's even possible to do so? If this describes you and your situation, then you aren't alone. Experian's 2015 VantageScore 3.0 data found that close to one-third of Americans have a credit score lower than 601 — and the good news is, there are ways to fix it.

Building good credit won't happen overnight because creating and maintaining a solid credit history takes time. You'll also need to accept the fact that it's going to take some hard work and patience to repair your credit.

The steps to fixing your credit and credit scores include getting a good sense of your finances. You will be going through them with a fine-toothed comb while looking for any errors and pinpointing problem areas, like overspending, that you need to address.

To fix your credit score:

Know your credit score and the balances of your credit cards or other credit accounts.

Find out which revolving accounts have the highest credit utilization (the amount of credit used versus the credit limit).

Pay extra attention to lowering the utilization of these accounts and focus on returning them to good standing to improve your credit.

Maintain healthy credit accounts and start building a positive credit history that will help you reach your personal goals. Find and begin to fix any negative items.

Keep in mind that credit age is also a factor in your credit score, so avoid closing too many accounts. This can hurt your efforts to fix your credit score.

It won't be easy, and it's certainly not as fun as going shopping, but the relief you'll feel at being able to take out new credit when you need it will be well worth the effort and time it took to rebuild your credit.

First Step: check your credit

The first thing you need to do is get your credit reports and credit scores from each of the credit bureaus so that you can gauge where you're at and determine what parts of your score need work.

You can get free copies of your credit reports from the three main credit bureaus — Experian, Equifax and TransUnion — once a year under the Fair Credit Reporting Act.

I recommend the following sites:

Identity Guard – "A powerful early warning system. Their state-of-the-art artificial intelligence capabilities continuously scour billions of data points to discover vulnerabilities and alert you when your identity may be at risk. Think of it as a "radar" that is always protecting your identity."

Identity theft affects 16.7 million Americans often with devastating consequences: loss of savings, being charged with a crime they didn't commit, even being held responsible for fraudulent medical claims.

Freecreditscore.com- "Credit resources. Whether you're looking to learn more about credit or simply trying to secure a better rate on credit cards or loans, freecreditscore.com has the resources to help you find what you're looking for."

NextAdvisor.com – "Credit monitoring. Your credit reports and credit scores determine whether you can get a home loan, an apartment, a credit card, a cell phone and much more. Yet most people don't even know their credit scores, or that they have more than one credit report. You can get your credit scores and see your credit reports by trying out any top-rated credit monitoring service, many of which offer free trials or money-back guarantees. In addition, these services give you explanations of what actions are helping or hurting your scores and what you can do to improve them. They'll also monitor your credit reports and scores daily for any changes and send you an alert through email or text when a change occurs."

You should get your credit reports from each of the major credit reporting agencies, as each may contain different data that could impact your scores. You'll rarely know ahead of time which report is being pulled by a lender, so it's important to make sure they're accurate and you've addressed any issues

What will I see on these reports?

You'll see basic details about yourself — your name, birthday, address, etc. It's important to review these to make sure they're accurate. Note: Past addresses may also be listed, which is OK.

You'll also see any financial legal issues you may have, like a bankruptcy, lien, judgment or wage garnishment. If one of these is bringing your credit scores down, take comfort in knowing these negative items eventually age off.

Beyond that is creditor information, which makes up most of your reports. This includes different accounts you have (loans, credit cards, etc.), their status (open/closed, in collections), balances, credit limits and payment details.

This may also include dates of missed payments or late payments, or when the accounts were sent to collections. From these details, your credit scores will be formed.

Credit scores are divided into five major categories:

➢ **Payment History** (35% of your scores) — Your history of repaying account debts

➢ **Credit Utilization** (30%) — How much debt you're carrying in relation to your credit limit

➢ **Length of Credit History** (15%) — How long you've had active credit accounts

➢ **Types of Credit** (10%) — Your variety of accounts

➢ **Credit Inquiries** (10%) — Number of inquiries into your credit profile

Now that you understand what these reports cover and how your credit scores are calculated, you can begin addressing your issues.

You can't fix bad credit in 30 days

I get it — you've found problems. Whether they're errors or areas you need to focus on, you may find yourself wanting results quickly. However, these revisions can't happen overnight. For instance, you can't lengthen your credit history right away.

You may be able to fix your credit utilization — the amount of debt you have relative to your credit limits and the second most principal factor in calculating your credit scores.

It's best to keep your credit utilization below 30% (ideally 10%) to show creditors you can manage your available credit responsibly without maxing out your credit cards.

If you went over that 30% mark, you can quickly undo any small drop you may have noticed in your credit scores by paying off those balances and getting your percentage back to less than 30% utilization.

Still, that's an exception to the rule. Some credit mistakes can impact your score for years. It's tough to hear, especially if you were really counting on that mortgage approval to finance your dream home.

Checking your credit on a regular basis is important. If you spot a mistake and can fix it before you apply, you can avoid that "Dear John" letter from a lender.

How long does it take to repair my credit?

If you have accurate negative information on your credit reports, then it can take a while for it to age off. Here's how long negative marks remain on your credit report:

- ➤ **Late Payments:** 7 years from the late payment date
- ➤ **Foreclosures:** 7 years
- ➤ **Collection Accounts:** 7 years and 180 days from the date of delinquency on the original debt
- ➤ **Short Sales:** 7 years
- ➤ **Bankruptcies:** 10 years from the filing date; 7 years for Chapter 13 cases
- ➤ **Repossessions:** 7 years
- ➤ **Judgments:** If the judgment has been paid, 7 or potentially longer if unpaid
- ➤ **Tax Liens:** 7 years after they are paid
- ➤ **Charge-Offs:** 7 years from the date the account was charged off

If you have inaccurate negative information on your credit reports, you can see some substantial changes to your credit scores as you work to fix them. Credit reporting agencies must respond to disputes within 30 days (some can take 45 days), which is much shorter than the years-long wait you'll face with accurate derogatory information.

If the credit reporting agency sides with you, they must remove the mistake immediately. In a 2012 Federal Trade Commission study on credit report accuracy, 79% of people who disputed an error on their credit reports were able to have it removed.

Steps to rebuild your credit

Remember, your path to better credit will vary significantly depending on your credit score problems. Here's how to rebuild it.

Pinpoint your credit-score killers

If you have one of those letters, we mentioned earlier that details your credit problems, you have some idea of what's holding you back. **Even though it may seem complex, as we mentioned, your credit score is based on five core factors: payment history, credit utilization, the age of credit accounts, the mix of credit accounts and history of applying for credit.** They're not equally weighted, and this information will most likely vary between credit bureaus.

Your **payment history** is the most important factor, accounting for **35%** of most scores. That's why even just one late payment can drop your score significantly.

Your **credit utilization** is the second biggest factor, accounting for **30%** of most scores. This encompasses the amount of revolving credit (i.e. credit cards, home equity lines of credit) you're using compared to the limits on those accounts.

The **age of your credit** accounts is another key factor, accounting for roughly **15%** of most credit scores. This is calculated by looking at the age of your oldest account and the average age of all your accounts. If this is hurting your scores, not much can be done except not closing the accounts.

The **mix of your credit** accounts, which accounts for **10%** of most credit scores, looks at how you handle different types of credit. There are two main types of credit — installment accounts (i.e. mortgages, car loans, student loans) and revolving accounts (i.e. credit cards and lines of credit).

Creditors want to see you can handle both kinds of credit responsibly. If you've only had credit cards in the past, a car loan or a mortgage may improve your credit score, but it's rarely a beneficial idea to take out a loan just to build credit.

The last major factor is your history of applying for credit. This accounts for 10% of most credit scores and may be holding you back if you applied for several credit accounts recently. This factor also takes time to correct, but any hard inquiries into your credit will only ding your scores slightly, and as they get older, they will have less of an impact. A year is generally when they begin to stop hurting your credit scores.

Now you know what's hurting your credit scores. So, what do you do? Since one of the fastest ways to see some improvement is by fixing errors on your credit report, that will be your next step.

Clean up your credit report

If you have mistakes on your credit report, you'll want to start the dispute process as soon as possible. Credit repair is something you can do on your own, or you can turn to the help of a professional credit repair company to help you fix your credit. Whichever option you choose, it's important to start right away.

As we explained earlier, credit reporting agencies have 30 days to respond (with some exceptions). You can read more about how to start the credit-dispute process here.

For now, here are some quick tips for determining how many credit repair letters you'll need to write or file online:

You need to dispute each mistake with each credit bureau. Just because the same mistake appears on all three credit reports doesn't mean disputing it with one of the bureaus will fix the others.

It's not uncommon to find multiple errors on your credit report, and you'll need to dispute each account separately. However, if you see multiple mistakes on the same account, you can group all those mistakes into one dispute.

You can dispute credit report errors without any experts' help, but for some people, the process is too confusing and they just want to hit the "easy" button. You can hire a credit repair company or law firm to represent you for a fee.

A good credit repair company will never promise a "300-point jump in your scores!" — In fact, that's illegal. They'll be upfront about what they can do and will take payment after they've delivered.

For more help, consider this sample credit repair letter.

Here's a sample letter you can use to write your disputes:

Example One:

Jane Q. Consumer

123 Main Street

Mainstreet, USA 12345

SSN: xxx-xx-1234

January 30, 2016

Ref #: 000-111-2222

To Whom It May Concern:

I've listed the unauthorized inquiries and fraudulent accounts below, so please delete the following inquires and fraudulent accounts from my credit report.

Under FDCPA Section 809 (b), you are not allowed to pursue collection activity until the debt is validated. Therefore, TransUnion, Experian or Equifax should be made aware the law. and Per the Fair Credit Reporting

Act, Section § 611 (a)(5), and know you have 30 days to investigate disputes.

Therefore, I prefer not to litigate until giving you time to correct the error, I will use the courts as needed to enforce my rights under the FDCPA. Under the Fair Debt Collection Practices Act Section 805 (C), it is my right to request that you cease contact with me.

This letter is a formal complaint that you are reporting inaccurate credit information. This letter is a formal request to remove unauthorized inquiries and fraudulent accounts from my credit report. I've listed the unauthorized inquiries and fraudulent accounts below so please delete the following inquiries from my credit report and under FDCPA Section 809 (b), you are not allowed to pursue collection activity until the debt is validated. Therefore, you should be made aware the law. and Per the Fair Credit Reporting Act, Section § 611 (a)(5), and know you have 30 days to investigate disputes.

Also, and under Section 611 (5)(A) of the FCRA – you are required to "...promptly DELETE all information which cannot be verified." The law is very clear as to the Civil liability and the remedy available to me for "negligent. Please be advised that under Section 611 (5) (A) of the

FCRA – you are required to "promptly DELETE all information which cannot be verified." The law is very clear as to the Civil liability and the remedy available to me (Section 616 & 617) if you fail to comply with Federal Law.

I demand the following accounts be verified or removed immediately.

Example Two:

Jane Q. Consumer

123 Main Street

Mainstreet, USA 12345

SSN: xxx-xx-1234

January 30, 2016

Ref #: 000-111-2222

To Whom It May Concern:

Please be advised this is my SECOND WRITTEN REQUEST. The unverified items listed below remain on my credit report in violation of Federal Law. You are required under the FCRA to have a copy of the original creditor's documentation on file to verify that this information is mine and is correct. In the results of your first investigation, you stated in writing that you "verified" that these items are being "reported correctly."

Who verified these accounts?

You have NOT provided me a copy of ANY original documentation required under Section 609 (a)(1)(A) & Section 611 (a)(1)(A) (a consumer contract with my signature on it) and under Section 611 (5)(A) of the FCRA – you are required to "…promptly DELETE all information which cannot be verified." The law is very clear as to the Civil liability and the remedy available to me for "negligent noncompliance" (Section 617) if you fail to comply. I am a litigious consumer and fully intend on pursuing litigation in this matter to enforce my rights under the FCRA.

I demand the following accounts be verified or removed immediately.

Example Three:

Jane Q. Consumer

123 Main Street

Mainstreet, USA 12345

SSN: xxx-xx-1234

January 30, 2016

Ref #: 000-111-2222

To Whom It May Concern:

Please be advised this is my THIRD WRITTEN REQUEST and FINAL WARNING that I fully intend to pursue litigation in accordance with the FCRA to enforce my rights and seek relief and recover all monetary damages that I may be entitled to under Section 616 and Section 617 regarding your continued willful and negligent noncompliance.

Despite two written requests, the unverified items listed below still remain on my credit report in violation of Federal Law. You are required under the FCRA to have a copy of the original creditors' documentation on file to verify that this information is mine and is correct. In the results of your first investigation and subsequent reinvestigation, you stated in writing that you "verified" that these items are being "reported correctly."

Who verified these accounts?

You have NOT provided me a copy of ANY original documentation (a consumer contract with my signature on it) as required under Section 609 (a)(1)(A) & Section 611 (a)(1)(A). Furthermore, you have failed to provide the method of verification as required under Section 611 (a) (7).

Please be advised that under Section 611 (5) (A) of the FCRA – you are required to "…promptly DELETE all information which cannot be verified." The law is very clear as to the Civil liability and the remedy available to me (Section 616 & 617) if you fail to comply with Federal Law. I am a litigious consumer and fully intend on pursuing litigation in this matter to enforce my rights under the FCRA.

Start some positive credit history

You may have been denied one kind of credit, but that doesn't mean you're shut out from borrowing entirely. If your payment history, credit utilization or a mix of accounts are hurting your scores, opening new credit may help you rebuild credit faster.

There are credit cards designed to help called secured credit cards. These require a deposit that generally serves as your credit limit. If you don't pay your bills, the card company can withdraw the deposit. If you open one of these cards, it's important to make on-time payments and keep an eye on your credit utilization.

Just because you have a card with a $1,000 limit doesn't mean you should charge $800 — that can hinder your efforts.

Benefits of a secured credit card to fix your credit

If you are an individual who has a very poor credit history or lacks credit history, then a secured credit card may be what you need to help repair your credit and raise your credit scores.

Depending on your situation, a secured credit card can start fixing your credit in as little as six months. However, it may take longer to see a marked improvement in some cases. If your credit history is lacking and you have no credit, then a secured card will be the best route because there is no negative information to start.

The secured credit card is a way to build and establish credit to obtain higher credit scores. If you found that you cannot get approved for a traditional credit card, you're still likely to get approved for a secured credit card because there is less risk for the lender. The card issuer will report to the credit bureaus about your ability to pay the credit card on time and how you manage and use the balance.

Additionally, the security deposit you used to obtain the card is used if you default on your payment. However, this is not the case if the defaulted balance happens to be higher than the security deposit amount. Using the security deposit means that even if you default, the card will be paid because it is secured by your funds and the account will not end up in collections due to nonpayment.

Here are some other quick tips to consider as you fix your credit:

Pay down credit card balances and refrain from making new purchases. In fact, you may want to put your plastic on ice.

If you're worried about taking out a credit card, consider a credit-builder loan with a bank or financial institution.

Refrain from closing old credit card accounts once you have them under control, as this can affect your credit utilization and make it harder to build a solid credit history.

When you're ready to shop for new credit like a mortgage or auto loan, rate shop during a 14- to 45-day window (depending on the scoring model). Most credit scoring models will group inquiries by type in that time frame.

Consider paying outstanding collection accounts. Some newer credit scoring models ignore paid collections entirely.

Why you should fix your credit

There are many reasons an individual should start on the path to credit repair. Some of the bigger reasons include the advantage of saving money on interest and no longer having to pay high security deposits. You may also be able to find lower insurance rates, receive higher credit limits, and stop debt collector harassment.

You will also see the beginning of a newfound financial freedom where you don't have to depend on co-signers to help you make purchases and secure loans. You will be relieved of the financial burden of inferior credit and will feel better about your repaired credit.

You won't find yourself crossing your fingers the next time a lender pulls your credit before you attempt to make a big purchase like buying a new house or car. You can sit there confident that you have a high score and you won't have to anxiously wait for the lender's rejection because of bad credit or the lack of credit.

Chapter Eleven:
Dispute an Error

How to dispute credit report errors

Found an error on your credit report? Don't freak out.
Federal law permits you to dispute credit report errors with
the credit bureau in question — and, chances are, there's a
"how to" section right there on the report containing the
error. If not, you can visit the credit bureau's website to get
the process started. The major credit reporting agencies
— Equifax, Experian and TransUnion — let you dispute an
error online. You should even be able to upload supporting
documentation when you file via their dispute portal.
(Note: You can also send the bureaus a written letter. Once
you formally dispute a line item, the credit bureau will have
30 to 45 days to investigate. If they determine the
information is, in fact, an error — or they can't verify it at
all — it will have to be removed. Of course, not all credit
report disputes go smoothly. Here's everything you need to
know in order to get inaccurate information off of your
credit file.

How common are credit report errors?

Believe it or not, finding an error on your credit report isn't an uncommon experience. In fact, a 2012 study from the Federal Trade Commission (Federal Trade Commission, n.d.) found that one in five Americans had an error on their credit reports. While some of those errors are innocuous — a misspelled name, perhaps, or an old address — others can kill your credit score, potentially costing you tens of thousands of dollars over your lifetime in higher interest rates, upfront deposits and increased insurance premiums.

Fortunately for consumers, the law is on their side. Credit bureaus have a responsibility to provide accurate information about consumers and are required to have a dispute process so consumers can get their credit reports fixed. Under the Fair Credit Reporting Act, which the FTC enforces, if you dispute an item on your credit report and the credit reporting agency cannot verify the item's accuracy or if the item is proven to be inaccurate, the item must be removed from your credit report 30 days after the dispute has been received by the bureau.

How credit report errors occur

Credit report errors can occur for a number of reasons. The National Consumer Law Center identified four common causes in a 2009 report on the topic.

Mixed Files. If someone with the same name or a similar name applies for credit, a piece of their file may become mixed with yours. A consumer with a common name like "John A. Smith," for example, could see his file mixed with a John B. Smith or a John A. Smith, Jr.

Identity theft. If someone has stolen your Social Security number, for example, they could open a new account in your name. This information could appear on your credit report and can be especially difficult to remove.

Furnisher Errors. There are three big players when it comes to credit report accuracy: credit bureaus, consumers and "data furnishers." That last one is important — it's the banks, lenders, debt collectors, and rental companies that supply (aka "furnish") the data that appears on your credit reports to the credit bureaus. Often, a furnisher can report something inaccurately, like a missed payment or a collection account that actually belongs to someone else.

Re-Aging of Old Debts. Certain debts have a ticking clock of sorts when it comes to your credit report. A collection account, for example, is supposed to age off of your credit report after seven years and 180 days from when it was first delinquent. However, sometimes "re-aging" occurs, often when a debt is sold to a third-party collector and the start date on that clock is muddied, causing your credit to take a hit much longer than it should under the law.

How to find out if you have derogatory marks on your credit report

Before you can fix the problem, you need to know what the problem is. You can either do this on your own or hire a credit repair company to manage the process for you.

You can get free copies of your credit reports once a year at AnnualCreditReport.com. Be sure to pull your reports from each of the major credit reporting agencies — again, that's Experian, Equifax and TransUnion. An error can exist on one report and not on the other two, and you never know which credit report will be used in a lending decision, so it's important to make sure all three reports are accurate.

Go through every section of each of your credit reports with a fine-toothed comb — there will likely be a lot of information there. If you see any accounts you don't recognize or late payments you think were on time, highlight them. You'll need to dispute each of those separately with the credit bureau who issued that report. Even if the same error appears on all three of your credit reports, you'll need to file three separate disputes over the item.

You can't make a blanket dispute claim for everything that's wrong on your report. Say, for example, that you have two collection accounts you want to dispute on the same credit report; here you'll need to file two separate disputes. However, if the disputes are for the same account — two late payments on your mortgage, for example — you only need to file one dispute, but you need to specify that you want both of the late payments removed. When you finish your credit report investigation, take stock of all the disputes you need to file. Depending on the number of inaccuracies on your credit report, the dispute process can be cumbersome.

Next up: How to actually get the items removed from your credit.

Steps to remove negative items from your credit

As we mentioned earlier, the dispute process can be done online or by mail with each of the credit reporting agencies.

You are now able to upload supporting documentation to each of the credit bureaus to challenge an error, but you can also include that information in your snail-mail letter if you decide to do so.

If sending your dispute by mail…

> ➤ Write a dispute letter. (We'll explain more on that in the next section.)
> ➤ Send it via certified mail so you can track when it was received.
> ➤ Include copies of any supporting documentation. Do not send originals!

You will hear back from the bureau regarding your dispute via U.S. mail, possibly after the 30-day window depending on how long it takes the letter to arrive at your address.

If sending your dispute online via one of the credit bureau portals…

> ➤ You don't need to write a formal letter, but you will need explain what the error is and where it appears on your report.
> ➤ You can submit it instantly to the bureau and can check the progress of your dispute online through a dispute portal.

The bureaus allow you to upload supporting documentation, which some people may prefer for security reasons versus sending sensitive information through the mail. You will be notified of the results by email.

When filing your dispute, make sure to clearly identify each mistake, articulate the facts and explain your reason for disputing the information, as the Consumer Financial Protection Bureau (CFPB) (Consumer Protection Act , 2018) notes on its site. You may consider enclosing a copy of your credit report with your claim and sending your letter of dispute by certified mail. Whatever you do, do not include the original copies of the documents you use to support your claim, the CFPB warns. The last thing you want is to lose your evidence.

Remember, the more evidence you have, the better your case may be. In some instances, it can be hard to determine what kinds of evidence are needed. For example, an identity theft victim may not know what they need to provide to show they didn't open an account in their name. After all, they never signed up for it! If you have reason to believe you were the victim of identity theft, the warning signs include mysterious addresses and accounts you never opened.

Unfortunately, this section is where many people opt to hit the "easy button" on their credit dispute process and simply give up. That's understandable, but you have options. You can hire a credit repair company to represent you on your behalf to the credit bureaus for a fee. A good credit repair company will explain exactly what it can and cannot do on your behalf, will never guarantee a "100-point rise in your credit score" (this is illegal, in fact), and will never ask for payment until after you've received services from them. Credit repair companies can be especially helpful if you have many errors on your credit report or have situations like a major identity theft issue or a divorce decree that potentially require more explanation and expertise to dispute. Some people just don't have the time to go through the whole dispute process and would prefer someone handle it for them instead.

How to write an effective dispute letter

If you want to take a DIY approach to credit repair, there are a few things you should remember when writing a dispute letter.

Be clear and concise. A credit bureau is concerned about accuracy, so pinpoint exactly what is inaccurate (the date of the inaccuracy, the account in question, the lender, etc.).

Don't quote federal laws. Writing that you want to initiate a dispute is sufficient enough. Credit bureaus know these laws already.

Include your return address so your results can be sent to the right place.

PROTECTING AMERICA'S CONSUMERS

Fair Debt Collection Practices Act

https://www.ftc.gov/enforcement/rules/rulemaking-regulatory-reform-proceedings/fair-debt-collection-practices-act-text

Truth in Lending Act

https://www.ftc.gov/enforcement/statutes/truth-lending-act

Fair Credit Billing Act

https://www.ftc.gov/enforcement/rules/rulemaking-regulatory-reform-proceedings/fair-credit-billing-act

Fair Credit Reporting Act

https://www.ftc.gov/consumer-protection/credit-reporting

https://www.federalregister.gov/documents/2011/12/21/2011-31728/fair-credit-reporting-regulation-v

https://en.wikipedia.org/wiki/Fair_Credit_Reporting_Act#Users_of_consumer_reports

FCRA § 605B (15 U.S.C. § 1681c-2)

Bureau addresses, websites and telephone
numbers to contact to dispute

**§ 605A. Identity theft prevention; fraud alerts
and active duty alerts [15 U.S.C. § 1681c-1]**
.................................26 § 605B.

**Block of information resulting from identity
theft [15 U.S.C. § 1681c-2]**

**§ 604. Permissible purposes of consumer reports
[15 U.S.C. § 1681b]** ....10 § 605.

**Requirements relating to information contained
in consumer reports [15 U.S.C. § 1681c].**

Relation State laws [15 U.S.C. § 1681t] ....

Statutes of limitations for each state (in number of years)

State	Written contracts	Oral contracts	Promissory notes	Open-ended accounts (including credit cards)
Alabama	6	6	6	3
Alaska	6	6	3	3
Arizona	5	3	6	3
Arkansas	5	3	3	3
California	4	2	4	4
Colorado	6	6	6	6
Connecticut	6	3	6	3
Delaware	3	3	3	4
D.C.	3	3	3	3
Florida	5	4	5	4

State	Written contracts	Oral contracts	Promissory notes	Open-ended accounts (including credit cards)
Georgia	6	4	6	4 or 6**
Hawaii	6	6	6	6
Idaho	5	4	5	5
Illinois	10	5	10	5
Indiana	10	6	10	6
Iowa	10	5	5	5
Kansas	5	3	5	3
Kentucky	10	5	15	5
Louisiana	10	10	10	3
Maine	6	6	6	6
Maryland	3	3	6	3
Massachusetts	6	6	6	6
Michigan	6	6	6	6

State	Written contracts	Oral contracts	Promissory notes	Open-ended accounts (including credit cards)
Minnesota	6	6	6	6
Mississippi	3	3	3	3
Missouri	10	5	10	5
Montana	8	5	8	5
Nebraska	5	4	5	4
Nevada	6	4	3	4
New Hampshire	3	3	6	3
New Jersey	6	6	6	6
New Mexico	6	4	6	4
New York	6	6	6	6
North Carolina	3	3	5	3
North Dakota	6	6	6	6

State	Written contracts	Oral contracts	Promissory notes	Open-ended accounts (including credit cards)
Ohio	6	15	15	6
Oklahoma	3	5	5	3
Oregon	6	6	6	6
Pennsylvania	4	4	4	4
Rhode Island	10	10	10	10
South Carolina	3	3	3	3
South Dakota	6	6	6	6
Tennessee	6	6	6	6
Texas	4	4	4	4
Utah	6	4	6	4
Vermont	6	6	5	3
Virginia	5	3	6	3

State	Written contracts	Oral contracts	Promissory notes	Open-ended accounts (including credit cards)
Washington	6	3	6	3
West Virginia	10	5	6	5
Wisconsin	6	6	10	6
Wyoming	10	8	10	8

Chapter Twelve:
Identity Theft

Identity theft is the deliberate use of someone else's identity, usually as a method to gain a financial advantage or obtain credit and other benefits in the other person's name, and perhaps to the other person's disadvantage or loss.

What should I do if I think my identity has been stolen?

If you become a victim of identity theft, or even suspect that you might be a victim, take immediate action. USA Identity Theft.

Affidavit form https://www.irs.gov/pub/irs-pdf/f14039.pdf

Form 14039 Can be downloaded from IRS.com at any time.

 Contact one of the credit reporting agencies' fraud alert departments and place a fraud alert on your credit report. This prevents identity thieves from opening accounts in your name. Many credit card companies offer no-cost fraud protection where you are not held financially responsible for charges made to your account by thieves who steal your personal information. In order to receive the most protection possible, though, it is important you call one of the credit reporting agencies as soon as you possibly can, even if you only suspect your identity has been stolen and aren't 100 percent sure.

Tell the agency you think your identity has been stolen. The agency will ask you to verify your identity with your Social Security number, name, address, and possibly other personal information.

One call does it all. The credit reporting agency you contacted must contact the other two. Each agency will place a fraud alert on their version of your credit report. For the next 90 days, your creditors and other businesses that want to offer you credit will see the alert on your credit report. If anyone asks for credit in your name, the appropriate lender will contact you to verify your identity and find out if you asked for credit.

Contact your lenders, banks, and insurance companies and let them know the situation. Ask to close accounts, and open new ones with new personal identification numbers (PINs) and passwords.

Victims of identity theft are entitled to a free credit report. Wait about a month before you request it. Some activity may take a while to show up on your report. Listed below are the changes you should watch out for.

- ➢ Personal information that has changed: your name, date of birth, Social Security number, address, and employer
- ➢ Inquiries from companies you didn't contact
- ➢ Accounts you didn't open
- ➢ Debts on your accounts you can't explain
- ➢ File a police report—it is proof of the crime. If the credit reporting agencies must investigate fraudulent activity on your report, they will need this police report.

Periodically check your credit reports over the next year to make sure no new fraudulent activity has occurred.

Work with the credit reporting agencies to remove fraudulent activities from your credit report.

Know your rights

"Here's an overview of your rights when recovering from identity theft. If someone is using your information to open new accounts or make purchases," report it and get help.

If someone steals your identity, you have the right to: create an FTC Identity Theft Report place a 90-day initial fraud alert on your credit report.

> ➢ Place a seven-year extended fraud alert on your credit report
> ➢ Get free copies of your credit reports
> ➢ Get fraudulent information removed (or "blocked") from your credit report
> ➢ dispute fraudulent or inaccurate information on your credit report
> ➢ Stop creditors and debt collectors from reporting fraudulent accounts
> ➢ Get copies of documents related to the identity theft
> ➢ Stop a debt collector from contacting you.

Documenting the theft

"You have the right to create an FTC Identity Theft Report. Your FTC Identity Theft Report proves to businesses that someone stole your identity, and makes it easier to correct problems caused by identity theft." You can create an FTC Identity Theft Report by filing a report with the FTC.

Working with credit bureaus

You have the right to: Place a 90-day initial fraud alert on your credit report. The fraud alert tells creditors that they must take reasonable steps to verify who is applying for credit in your name. To place this alert, contact one of the three national credit bureaus: Equifax, TransUnion, or Experian. The one you contact must notify the others.

When you place an initial fraud alert, you're also entitled to a free copy of your credit reports. You'll get a confirmation letter from each credit bureau with instructions for how to get your free reports.

Place a seven-year extended fraud alert on your credit report. To do this, send a copy of your FTC Identity Theft Report to each credit bureau. The extended fraud alert means potential creditors must contact you before they issue credit in your name. In your letter, be sure to give the best way for a creditor to reach you.

Each credit bureau will send you a letter confirming that they placed an extended fraud alert on your file. That letter also will include instructions on how to get free copies of your credit report.

Get credit bureaus to remove fraudulent information from your credit report. This is called blocking. You must send them a copy of your FTC Identity Theft Report, proof of your identity, and a letter stating which information is fraudulent. Then the credit bureau must tell the relevant creditor that someone stole your identity. Creditors cannot turn fraudulent debts over to debt collectors.

Dispute fraudulent or inaccurate information on your credit report. Do this by writing to the credit bureau. They must investigate your dispute and amend your report if you are right.

In many states, you have the right to place a freeze on your credit report. A credit freeze makes it less likely that an identity thief could open a new account in your name.

Communicating with creditors and debt collectors

You have the right to stop creditors and debt collectors from reporting fraudulent accounts. After you give them a copy of a valid FTC Identity Theft Report, they may not report fraudulent accounts to the credit reporting companies.

Get copies of documents related to the theft of your identity, like transaction records or applications for new accounts. Write to the company that has the documents, and include a copy of your FTC Identity Theft Report. You also can tell the company to give the documents to a specific law enforcement agency.

Stop debt collectors from contacting you. In most cases, debt collectors must stop contacting you after you send them a letter telling them to stop.

Get written information from a debt collector about a debt, including the name of the creditor and the amount you supposedly owe. If a debt collector contacts you about a debt, request this information in writing.

Limits on financial losses

You have limited liability for fraudulent debts caused by identity theft.

Under most state laws, you're not responsible for any debt incurred on fraudulent new accounts opened in your name without your permission.

Under federal law, the amount you have to pay for unauthorized use of your credit card is limited to $50. If you report the loss to the credit card company before your credit card is used by a thief, you aren't responsible for any unauthorized charges.

If your ATM or debit card is lost or stolen, you can limit your liability by reporting the loss immediately to your bank or credit union.

If you report your debit card lost:	Your maximum loss is:
Before any unauthorized charges are made.	$0
Within 2 business days after you learn about the loss or theft.	$50
More than 2 business days after you learn about the loss or theft, but less than 60 calendar days after your statement is sent to you.	$500
More than 60 calendar days after your statement is sent to you.	Possibly unlimited

If someone makes unauthorized debits to your bank or credit union account using your debit card number (not your card), you aren't responsible – if you report the problem within 60 days after they send your account statement showing the unauthorized debits.

Most state laws limit your liability for fraudulent checks issued on your bank or credit union account if you notify the bank or credit union promptly.

Other federal rights

Under the justice for all act, you have additional rights when the identity thief is criminally prosecuted in federal court. You have the right to: reasonable protection from the accused reasonable, accurate, and timely notice about any public court proceeding, parole proceeding involving the crime, or release or escape of the accused not be excluded from any public court proceeding unless the judge decides that your testimony would change significantly if you heard other testimony be reasonably heard at any public proceeding in the district court that involves release, plea, sentencing, or parole confer with the attorney for the government in the case full and timely restitution as provided in the law proceedings free from unreasonable delay be treated with fairness and respect for your dignity and privacy.

State rights

In many states, businesses or organizations that lose or misplace certain types of personal information must tell you if that has happened. To learn more, check with <u>your state and local consumer protection offices</u>.

Credit Fraud Prevention Kit

**Stop Fraud Before It Happens –
Control the Damage if it Does**

Know your credit report

Monitoring your credit is the first step in preventing fraud. Order your credit report at least once a year and immediately report any unfamiliar accounts or charges.

Your rights under the FACT Act

The Fair and Accurate Credit Transactions (FACT) Act was signed into law in December 2003. This law incorporates new privacy regulations, identity theft protection, dispute procedures and the distribution of free annual Personal Credit Reports. This means that you can review a free copy of your Personal Credit Report every 12 months. You can request your FACT Act Personal Credit Reports from each of the credit reporting agencies online at **www.annualcreditreport.com.** You can also submit your request by calling (877) 322-8228 or by mail (see details online).

Guard your identity

Destroy credit card and bank statements, credit card offers, and credit card receipts before discarding. Carry only the identification and credit cards you need that day. Never carry social security cards, birth certificates, or passports unless you have to. Don't print your social security number on your driver's license.

Memorize PINs and passwords

Don't write down or carry PINs or passwords with you. Choose a password or PIN that's easy to remember, and memorize it. But be careful to avoid obvious passwords like birthdays, phone numbers, or addresses.

Avoid credit repair scams. So-called "credit repair" companies can't do anything to repair your credit other than what you could do yourself. All they can do is dispute information contained on your report and have inaccuracies corrected for no charge. However, they often use deceptive or even litigate practices. If you believe a credit repair company is breaking the law, report them to your state authorities and the FTC.

Protect your information

Keep a copy of all account information, including account numbers, expiration dates, and telephone numbers for fraud departments and customer service in a secure place. Never disclose social security numbers or other personal information over the telephone or internet unless it is to a trusted source.

Watch for the signs

The sooner you detect credit fraud, the less damage it can do. Know the warning signs and be ready to act. Watch for missing statements or bills, unusual charges on your accounts, incoming letters informing you that you've been approved or denied credit you didn't apply for, or bills and statements you don't recognize.

Act quickly if you have any reason to suspect credit fraud; contact banks, creditors, and the three main credit information providers immediately.

Remember, you're entitled to copies of your report at no charge if you think you have been the victim of identity theft:

Steps to recover from credit fraud

Step 1: Add fraud alert

Have TransUnion add an initial, extended, or active duty fraud alert to your credit file advising potential creditors to contact you personally before approving any applications made in your name. You only need to make a single request, and they will automatically inform the other two national credit reporting agencies.

Step 2: Inspect your credit reports

Visit www.transunion.com or call (800) 680-7289 to request your report. Dispute all information that you don't recognize. Provide a copy of your police report, a notarized FTC fraud affidavit, or other relevant documentation of proof with your dispute.

Step 3: Report the fraud

Notify your local, state, and federal law enforcement offices immediately. Be sure to request a case number and a copy of the police report to provide TransUnion's Fraud Victim Assistance Department.

Step 4: Contact credit financial institutions

Notify your credit institutions and banks as soon as possible. Document the fraud to avoid responsibility for fraudulent debts. Keep a log of all phone conversations, including names of people with whom you spoke.

Consumer Resources

Fraud Victim Assistance Department (800) 580-7289

United State Court Locator

http://www.uscourts.gov/court-locatorwebsite for the U.S. Trustee.

United State Bankruptcy

http://www.uscourts.gov/services-forms/bankruptcy

Identity Protection https://www.identityguard.com/

Free Credit Scores https://www.freecreditscore.com/

Social Security Administration https://www.ssa.gov/

US Passport Division

https://travel.state.gov/content/travel/en/passports.html

Department of Motor Vehicle https://www.dmvusa.com/

US Post Office Mail Fraud

https://postalinspectors.uspis.gov/investigations/MailFraud/MailFraud.aspx

Federal Housing Administration

https://fhagovernmentloans.org/index.htm

US Department of Education https://www.ed.gov/

US Student Loans

https://studentloans.gov/myDirectLoan/index.action

IRS https://irs.gov

Equifax
Fraud Department P.O. Box 740256 Atlanta,
GA1O374(800) 525-6285
Call 1-800-525-6285
Visit www.equifax.com

Experian
Fraud Department Box 2002 Allen, TX 75013 (888) 397-
3742
Call 1-888-397-3742
Visit www.experian.com

TransUnion
Fraud Department P.O. Box 2000 P.O. Chester, PA 19016
(800) 680-7289
Call 1-800-680-7289
Visit http://www.transunion.com

Federal Trade Commission https://www.ftc.gov/

Fair Debt Collection Practices Act

https://www.ftc.gov/enforcement/rules/rulemaking-regulatory-reform-proceedings/fair-debt-collection-practices-act-text

Truth in Lending Act

https://www.ftc.gov/enforcement/statutes/truth-lending-act

Fair Credit Billing Act

https://www.ftc.gov/enforcement/rules/rulemaking-regulatory-reform-proceedings/fair-credit-billing-act

Fair Credit Reporting Act

https://www.ftc.gov/consumer-protection/credit-reporting

https://www.federalregister.gov/documents/2011/12/21/2011-31728/fair-credit-reporting-regulation-v

State Consumer Protection Offices-

https://www.usa.gov/state-consumer

History of Credit Bureaus

Equifax Inc. "is a consumer credit reporting agency. Equifax collects and aggregates information on over 800 million individual consumers and more than 88 million businesses worldwide. Founded in 1899 and based in Atlanta, Georgia, it is one of the three largest credit agencies along with Experian and TransUnion (known as the "Big Three"). Equifax has US$3.1 billion in annual revenue and 9,000+ employees in 14 countries. It is listed on the NYSE as EFX.

Aside from offering credit and demographic related data and services to business, Equifax sells credit monitoring and fraud-prevention services directly to consumers. Like all credit reporting agencies, the company is required by US law to provide consumers with one free credit report every year.

Equifax was founded by Cator and Guy Woolford in Atlanta, GA, as Retail Credit Company in 1899. The company grew quickly and by 1920 had offices throughout the US and Canada. By the 1960s, Retail Credit Company was one of the nation's largest credit bureaus, holding files on millions of American and Canadian citizens. Even though the company continued to do credit reporting, the majority of their business was making reports to insurance companies when people applied for new insurance policies including life, auto, fire and medical insurance. All of the major insurance companies used RCC to get information on health, habits, morals, use of vehicles and finances. They also investigated insurance claims and made employment reports when people were seeking new jobs. Most of the credit work was then being done by a subsidiary, Retailers Commercial Agency.

Retail Credit Company's extensive information holdings, and its willingness to sell them to anyone, attracted criticism of the company in the 1960s and 1970s. Complaints included that it collected "...facts, statistics, inaccuracies and rumors… about virtually every phase of a person's life; his marital troubles, jobs, school history, childhood, sex life, and political activities." The company was also alleged to reward its employees for collecting negative information on consumers.

As a result, when the company moved to computerize its records, which would lead to much wider availability of the personal information it held, the US Congress held hearings in 1970. These led to the enactment of the Fair Credit Reporting Act in the same year which gave consumers rights regarding information stored about them in corporate databanks. It is alleged that the hearings prompted the Retail Credit Company to change its name to Equifax in 1975 to improve its image.

The company later expanded into commercial credit reports on companies in the US, Canada and the UK, where it came into competition with companies such as Dun & Bradstreet and Experian. The insurance reporting was phased out. The company also had a division selling specialist credit information to the insurance industry but spun off this service, including the Comprehensive Loss Underwriting Exchange (CLUE) database as ChoicePoint in 1997. The company previously offered digital certification services, which it sold to GeoTrust in September 2001. In the same year, Equifax spun off its payment services division, forming the publicly listed company Certegy, which subsequently acquired Fidelity National Information Services in 2006. Certegy effectively became a subsidiary of Fidelity National Financial as a result of this reverse acquisition merger (See Certegy and

Fidelity National Information Services for further information).

In October 2010, Equifax was acquired Anakam, an identity verification software company.

Equifax purchased eThority, a business intelligence (BI) company headquartered in Charleston, South Carolina in October 2011.

Equifax Workforce Solutions is one of the 55 contractors hired by the United States Department of Health and Human Services to work on the HealthCare.gov web site.

For most of its existence, Equifax has operated primarily in the business-to-business sector, selling consumer credit and insurance reports and related analytics to businesses in a range of industries. Business customers include retailers, insurance firms, healthcare providers, utilities, government agencies, as well as banks, credit unions, personal and specialty finance companies and other financial institutions. Equifax sells businesses credit reports, analytics, demographic data, and software. Credit reports provide detailed information on the personal credit and payment history of individuals, indicating how they have honored financial obligations such as paying bills or repaying a loan. Credit grantors use this information to decide what sort of products or services to offer their customers, and on what terms. Equifax also provides commercial credit reports, similar to Dun & Bradstreet, containing financial and non-financial data on businesses of all sizes. Equifax collects and provides data through the NCTUE, an exchange of non-credit data including consumer payment history on telco and utility accounts.

In 1999, Equifax began offering services to the credit consumer sector, such as credit fraud and identity theft prevention products. Equifax and other credit monitoring agencies are required by law to provide US residents with one free credit file disclosure every 12 months; the Annualcreditreport.com website incorporates data from US Equifax credit records.

In 2016, Equifax partnered with CreditMantri, a credit facilitator based in Chennai, to offer free credit score and loan reports to its customers.

Equifax also offers fraud prevention products based on device fingerprinting such as the "FraudIQ Authenticate Device." **Equifax.com**

Experian plc "is a consumer credit reporting agency. Experian collects and aggregates information on over one billion people and businesses including 235 million individual US consumers and more than 25 million US businesses. Based in Dublin, Ireland, the company operates in 37 countries with headquarters in the United Kingdom, the United States, and Brazil. The company employs approximately 17,000 people and reported revenue for 2018 of US $4.6 billion. It is listed on the London Stock Exchange and is a constituent of the FTSE 100 Index. Experian is a partner in the UK government's Verify ID system and USPS Address Validation. It is one of the "Big Three" credit-reporting agencies, alongside TransUnion and Equifax.

In addition to its credit services, Experian also sells decision analytics and marketing assistance to businesses, including individual fingerprinting and targeting. Its consumer services include online access to credit history and products meant to protect from fraud and identity theft. Like all credit reporting agencies, the company is required by US law to provide consumers with one free credit report every year.

The company was established in the United States as TRW Information Systems and Services Inc., a subsidiary of TRW Inc., when it acquired Credit Data in 1968. In November 1996, TRW sold the unit, as Experian, to two Boston private equity firms: Bain Capital and Thomas H. Lee Partners. Just one month later, the two firms sold Experian to The Great Universal Stores Limited, a retail conglomerate with millions of customers paying for goods on credit based in Manchester, England (later renamed GUS).

The Great Universal Stores Limited employed John Peace, a computer programmer, to combine the mail order data from its various subsidiaries and businesses to create a central database to which was later added electoral roll data as well as county court judgements. GUS's database was commercialized in 1980 under the name Commercial Credit Nottingham (CCN). So, when The Great Universal Stores Limited acquired Experian in 1996, Experian was merged into CCN.

Over the next ten years, Experian broadened its product range to new industry sectors beyond financial services, and entered new markets such as Latin America, Asia Pacific and Eastern Europe. The business expanded through both organic development and acquisitions. In October 2006, Experian was demerged from the British company GUS and listed on the London Stock Exchange.

In August 2005, Experian accepted a settlement with the Federal Trade Commission (FTC) over charges that Experian had violated a previous settlement with the FTC. The FTC's allegations concerned customers who signed up for the "free credit report" at Experian's Consumerinfo.com site. The FTC alleged that ads for the "free credit report" did not adequately disclose that Experian would automatically enroll customers in Experian's $79.95 credit-monitoring program.

In August 2010, Experian became the first CICRA licensed credit bureau to go live in India. Since then the company has provided Experian credit reports to lenders and consumers in compliance with the Reserve Bank of India's (RBI) guidelines.

Experian purchased a majority stake in Techlightenment on 17 January 2011, as part of Experian's strategy to grow its digital marketing capabilities. Techlightenment is a data driven technology and marketing company based in the UK, which helps clients to leverage advertising through key social media platforms. Techlightenment forms part of the UK Experian Marketing Services Division.

In May 2011, Experian acquired a 98% holding in Computec S.A., a credit services information provider based in Colombia, for the equivalent of $380m USD.

In June 2011, Experian acquired Medical Present Value, Inc. (MPV), a provider of data, analytics and software in the US healthcare payments market. Its products are used by healthcare providers to manage payments between patients, commercial payers (such as insurance companies).

In July 2011, Experian acquired Virid Interatividade Digital Ltda ("Virid"), an email marketing company offering email delivery, email based behavioral segmentation, real-time campaign reporting, mobile delivery and social media integration in Brazil.

In December 2011, Experian acquired Garlik Ltd, a provider of web monitoring services in the UK. Garlik helps consumers to protect themselves from the risks of identity theft and financial fraud.

In May 2012, Experian announced it had signed an agreement to sell PriceGrabber, its price comparison shopping business and North American online lead generation activities, which operate under the brands Classes USA and LowerMyBills, to Ybrant Digital Limited, a digital marketing services business based in Hyderabad, India. However, since then, Experian has announced that Ybrant Digital has failed to comply with its obligation to close the transaction and Experian considers Ybrant Digital to be in breach of contract.

In February 2013 Experian launched its consumer credit bureau in Australia where it provides consumer credit reports to utility, financial and telecommunication companies. This launch follows the passing of the Privacy Amendment Bill in November 2012, which means a step change for lenders, who are now able to take positive (in addition to negative) credit history into account when making lending decisions.

In October 2013, Experian bought 41st Parameter, a fraud-prevention vendor, increasing its presence in the fraud prevention market and extending its presence into web fraud transaction protection. Then in November 2013, Experian bought Passport Health Communications, a data and software provider, enabling it to offer clients in the US healthcare industry a one-stop-shop to manage risk and to satisfy their payments requirements.

In October 2017, Experian in North America acquired Clarity Services, a leading credit bureau servicing the sub-prime market. That meant the acquisition of unique credit data and insights into over 60m individuals. New Clarity Services products were added to the traditional bureau with the introduction of the first new product which combined data from both Clarity and Experian to enhance credit risk decisions.

In March 2018, Experian launched the new identity protection proposition in the US, substantially developed the credit comparison services and agreed upon the acquisition of ClearScore (6m users, mainly younger, digitally savvy consumers), which added complementary credit comparison brand in the UK.

Like the other major credit reporting bureaus, Experian is chiefly regulated in the United States by the Fair Credit Reporting Act (FCRA). The Fair and Accurate Credit Transactions Act of 2003, signed into law in 2003, amended the FCRA to require the credit reporting companies to provide consumers with one free copy of their credit report per 12-month period. Like its main competitors, TransUnion and Equifax, Experian markets credit reports directly to consumers. Experian heavily markets its for-profit credit reporting service, FreeCreditReport.com, and all three agencies have been criticized and even sued for selling credit reports that can be obtained at no cost.

Its market segmentation tool, Mosaic, is used by political parties to identify groups of voters. In the British version there are 15 main groups, broken down into 89 hyper-specific categories, from "corporate chieftains" to "golden empty-nesters" which can be taken down to the level of individual postcodes. It was first used by the Labor Party, but then taken up by the Conservatives in the 2015 General Election campaign." **Experian.com**

TransUnion "is a consumer credit reporting agency. TransUnion collects and aggregates information on over one billion individual consumers in over thirty countries including "200 million files profiling nearly every credit-active consumer in the United States." Its customers include over 65,000 businesses. Based in Chicago, Illinois, TransUnion's 2014 revenue was $1.3 billion US. It is the smallest of the three largest credit agencies, along with Experian and Equifax (known as the Big Three).

TransUnion also markets credit reports and other credit and fraud-protection products directly to consumers. Like all credit reporting agencies, the company is required by US law to provide consumers with one free credit report every year.

TransUnion was originally formed in 1968 as a holding company for the railroad leasing organization, Union Tank Car Company. The following year, it acquired the Credit Bureau of Cook County, which possessed and maintained 3.6 million card files. In 1981, a Chicago-based holding company, The Marmon Group, acquired TransUnion for approximately $688 million. Almost thirty years later, in 2010, Goldman Sachs Capital Partners and Advent International acquired it from Madison Dearborn Partners.

In 2014, TransUnion acquired Hank Asher's data company TLO. On June 25, 2015, TransUnion became a publicly traded company for the first time, trading under the symbol TRU.

TransUnion has evolved its business over the years to offer products and services for both businesses and consumers. For businesses, TransUnion has changed its traditional credit score offering to include trended data that helps predict consumer repayment and debt behavior. This product, referred to as Credit Vision, launched in October 2013.

Its Smart Move™ service facilitates credit and background checks for consumers who may be serving in a landlord capacity.

In September 2013, the company acquired eScan Data Systems of Austin to provide post-service eligibility determination support to hospitals and healthcare systems. The technology was integrated into TransUnion's ClearIQ platform which tracks patients' demographic and insurance related information to support benefit verification.

In November 2013, TransUnion acquired TLO LLC, a company that leverages data in support of its investigative and risk management tools. Its TLOxp technology aggregates data sets and uses a proprietary algorithm to uncover relationships between data that were not possible before.

In 2014, a TransUnion analysis found that reporting rental payment information to credit bureaus can positively affect credit scores. To benefit consumers, they initiated a service called Resident Credit, making it easy for property owners to report data about their tenants to TransUnion on a monthly basis. These reports include the amount each tenant pays, the timeliness of their last payment, and any remaining balance the tenant currently owes. As a result, companies have started reporting rent payment information to TransUnion, including YapStone, Inc., Pangea Real Estate, and Rent Reporters.

As part of its fraud protection products, it also offers businesses a tool called Decision Edge that aggregates the data needed to prevent fraud through a system that customizes the information needed to finalize a transaction.

For consumers, TransUnion offers credit monitoring and identity theft protection tools. The company's app offers a function called CreditLock that allows an individual to unlock and lock their credit to help protect against fraudulent activity." **TransUnion.com**

Glossary

Account Condition: Indicates the present state of the account, but does not indicate the payment history of the account that led to the current state (i.e. open, paid, charge-off, repossession, settled, foreclosed, etc.).

Account Number: The unique number assigned by a creditor to identify your account with them. Experian removes several digits from each account number on the credit report as a fraud prevention measure.

Accounts in Good Standing: Credit items that have a positive status and should reflect favorably on your creditworthiness.

Adjustment: Percentage of the debt that is to be repaid to the credit grantors in a Chapter 13 bankruptcy.

AKA: Also known as

Annual Fee: Credit card issuers often (but not always) require you to pay a special charge once a year for the use of their service, usually between $15 and $55.

Annual Percentage Rate (APR): A measure of how much interest credit will cost you, expressed as an annual percentage.

Authorized User: A person permitted by a credit cardholder to charge goods and services on the cardholder's account but who is not responsible for repayment of the debt. The account displays on the credit reports of the cardholder as well as the authorized user. If you wish to have your name permanently removed as an authorized user on an account, you will need to notify the credit grantor.

Account Rating: There are standard codes set by the credit reporting industry, which the creditors use when they provide this information to the credit bureaus. The credit bureaus only report what is provided to them and do not determine the rating. Here is a breakdown of the ratings:

➤ A new account which is "too new to rate" is rated 0.

➤ An account that is paid on time and is the best rating is "pays as agreed" and rated 1.

➤ An account that is 30 days late, which is considered 30 to 59 days past due, is rated 2.

➤ An account that is 60 days late, which is 60 to 89 days past due, is rated 3.

➢ An account that is 90 days late, which is 90 to 119 days past due, is rated 4

➢ An account that is 120 days late, which is 120 to 149 days past due, is rated 5.

➢ Regular payments agreed upon under a wage earner plan is rated 6.

➢ Repossession is rated 8.

➢ Bad debt or a collection is rated 9.

Account Classification: Account Classification. Most general ledger accounts have a classification; all Assets, Liability, and Equity accounts MUST have a classification. The classification is used for a number of purposes.

➢ **Asset**
➢ **Liability**
➢ **Equity**
➢ **Revenue**
➢ **Expenses**

Account: An account is a record in the general ledger that is used to collect and store debit and credit amounts. An amount of money deposited with a bank, as in checking or savings.

Balloon Payments: A loan with a balloon payment requires that a single, lump-sum payment be made at the end of the loan.

Bankruptcy Code: Federal laws governing the conditions and procedures under which persons claiming inability to repay their debts can seek relief.

Credit Analysis: Credit analysis is a type of analysis an investor or bond portfolio manager performs on companies or other debt issuing entities to measure the entity's ability to meet its debt obligations. The credit analysis seeks to identify the appropriate level of default risk associated with investing in that particular entity.

Credit Capacity: This is how much credit you are able to handle. In deciding whether you qualify for a particular loan, your income is considered along with any other expenses and debts you may have.

Credit Grantor: The credit grantor is another term used to describe your credit card issuer, or the company that has granted credit to you.

Credit History: A credit history is a record of a borrower's responsible repayment of debts. A credit report is a record of the borrower's credit history from a number of sources, including banks, credit card companies, collection agencies, and governments.

Credit Reference: A credit reference is information, the name of an individual, or the name of an organization that can provide details about an individual's past track record with credit. Credit rating agencies provide credit references for companies while credit bureaus provide credit references for individuals.

Certificate of Deposit: A certificate issued by a bank to a person depositing money for a specified length of time.

Consumer Reporting Agency or Credit Bureau: A credit bureau is a collection agency that gathers account information from various creditors and provides that information to a consumer reporting agency in the United States, a credit reference agency in the United Kingdom, a credit reporting body in Australia, a credit information company (CIC) in India, a Special Accessing Entity in the Philippines, and also to private lenders.

Credit Stability: Credit stability is an intrinsic characteristic of a credit or a sector and should not be confused with rating stability. Ratings represent our forward-looking view on creditworthiness, and they migrate in line with any change in our view on credit conditions or expectations.

Capacity: This is a factor in determining creditworthiness. Capacity is assessed by weighing a borrower's earning ability and the likelihood of continuing income against the amount of debt the borrower carries at the time the application for credit is made. While capacity may be considered in a credit decision, the credit report does not contain information about earning ability or the likelihood of continuing income.

Civil Judgement: A civil judgment refers to a ruling made by a court during a lawsuit. In many cases, people have judgments because of unpaid collections or other financial obligations. These judgments show up on your credit report as a public record placed there by the credit bureaus.

Chapter 7 Bankruptcy: The chapter of the Bankruptcy Code that provides for court administered liquidation of the assets of a financially troubled individual or business.

Chapter 11 Bankruptcy: The chapter of the Bankruptcy Code that is usually used for the reorganization of a financially troubled business. Used as an alternative to liquidation under Chapter 7. The U.S. Supreme Court has held that an individual may also use Chapter 11.

Chapter 12 Bankruptcy: The chapter of the Bankruptcy Code adopted to address the financial crisis of the nation's farming community. Cases under this chapter are administered like Chapter 11 cases, but with special protections to meet the special conditions of family farm operations.

Chapter 13 Bankruptcy: The chapter of the Bankruptcy Code in which debtors repay debts according to a plan accepted by the debtor, the creditors and the court. Plan payments usually come from the debtor's future income and are paid to creditors through the court system and the bankruptcy trustee.

Charge-off: The action of transferring accounts deemed uncollectible to a category such as bad debt or loss. Collectors will usually continue to solicit payments, but the accounts are no longer considered part of a company's receivable or profit picture.

Civil Action: Any court action against a consumer to regain money for someone else. Usually it will be a wage assignment, child support judgment, small claims judgment or a civil judgment.

Claim Amount: The amount awarded in a court action.

Closed Date: The date an account was closed.

Co-maker: A creditworthy co-maker is sometimes required in situations where an applicant's qualifications are marginal. A co-maker is legally responsible to repay the charges in the joint account agreement.

Cosigner: A person who pledges in writing as part of a credit contract to repay the debt if the borrower fails to do so. The account displays on both the borrower's and the cosigner's credit reports.

Credit Limit/Line of Credit: In open-end credit, this is the maximum amount a borrower can draw upon or the maximum that an account can show as outstanding.

Credit Items: Information reported by current or past creditors.

Credit Report: A confidential report on a consumer's payment habits as reported by their creditors to a consumer credit reporting agency. The agency provides the information to credit grantors who have a permissible purpose under the law to review the report.

Credit Scoring: A tool used by credit grantors to provide an objective means of determining risks in granting credit. Credit scoring increases efficiency and timely response in the credit granting process. Credit scoring criteria are set by the credit grantor.

Creditworthiness: The ability of a consumer to receive favorable consideration and approval for the use of credit from an establishment to which they applied.

Docket Number: In general, courts assign each newly filed action with a docket number, which often refers to the year in which the case was commenced followed by a sequential reference number, and sometimes includes letters or numbers indicating the type (civil, criminal, family court, etc.) or location of filing and/or the initials.

Defendant: An individual, company, or institution sued or accused in a court of law.

Date Filed: The date that a public record was awarded.

Date of Status: This is the date the creditor last updated the account. This date does not affect how long an account remains on the report and should not be confused with the "Original Delinquency Date."

Date Opened: On the credit report, this indicates the date an account was opened.

Date Resolved: The completion date or satisfaction date of a public record item.

Delinquent: Accounts classified into categories according to the time past due. Common classifications are 30, 60, 90 and 120 days past due. Special classifications also include charge-off, repossession, transferred, etc.

Discharge: This is granted by the court to release a debtor from most of their debts that were included in a bankruptcy. Any debts not included in the bankruptcy – alimony, child support, liability for willful and malicious conduct and certain student loans – cannot be discharged.

Disclosure: Providing the consumer with his or her credit history as required by the FCRA. Experian provides consumer credit report disclosures via the Internet, by U.S. Mail or in person at their office location in Santa Ana, CA.

Dismissed: When a consumer files a bankruptcy, the judge may decide to not allow the consumer to continue with the bankruptcy. If the judge rules against the petition, the bankruptcy is known as dismissed.

Dispute: If a consumer believes an item on their credit report is inaccurate or incomplete, they may challenge or dispute the item. Experian will investigate and correct or remove any inaccurate information or information that cannot be verified. Experian gives consumers the option of disputing online or they may call the telephone number on their credit report for assistance.

ECOA: Standard abbreviation for Equal Credit Opportunity Act.

End-user: The business that receives the report for decision making purposes that meet the permissible purpose requirements of the FCRA.

Equal Credit Opportunity Act (ECOA): A federal law which prohibits creditors from discriminating against credit applicants on the basis of sex, marital status, race, color, religion, age, and/or receipt of public assistance.

Equifax: One of the three national credit reporting agencies, headquartered in Atlanta, Ga. The other two are Experian and TransUnion.

Experian: One of the three national credit reporting agencies, with U.S. headquarters in Costa Mesa, CA. The other two are Equifax and TransUnion.

Foreclosure: Foreclosure is a legal process in which a lender attempts to recover the balance of a loan from a borrower who has stopped making payments to the lender by forcing the sale of the asset used as the collateral for the loan.

Fair Credit and Charge Card Disclosure Act: Amendments to the Truth in Lending Act that require the disclosure of the costs involved in credit card plans that are offered by mail, telephone or applications distributed to the general public.

Fair Credit Billing Act: Federal legislation that provides a specific error resolution procedure to protect credit card customers from making payments on inaccurate billings.

Fair Credit Reporting Act (FCRA): Federal legislation governing the actions of credit reporting agencies.

Fair Debt Collection Practices Act (FDCPA): Federal legislation prohibiting abusive and unfair debt collection practices.

Finance Charge: The amount of interest. Finance charges are usually included in the monthly payment total.

First Reported: The date when the first account status was reported by the account holder.

Fixed Rate: An annual percentage rate that does not change.

Grace Period: The time period you have to pay a bill in full and avoid interest charges.

Guarantor: The person responsible for paying a bill.

History Payment: A payment history is an indication for lenders and creditors whether an individual is a lending risk due to a history of late or missed payments.

High Balance: The highest amount that you have owed on an account to date.

Installment Credit: Credit accounts in which the debt is divided into amounts to be paid successively at specified intervals.

Interest: Money paid regularly at a particular rate for the use of money lent, or for delaying the repayment of a debt.

Investigation: The process a consumer credit reporting agency goes through in order to verify credit report information disputed by a consumer. The credit grantor who supplied the information is contacted and asked to review the information and report back; they will tell the credit reporting agency that the information is accurate as it appears, or they will provide corrected information to update the report.

Investigative Consumer Reports: These are consumer reports that are usually done for background checks, security clearances and other sensitive jobs. An investigative consumer report might contain information obtained from a credit report, but it is more comprehensive than a credit report. It contains subjective material on an individual's character, habits and lifestyle, which is obtained through interviews of associates. Experian does not provide investigative consumer reports.

Involuntary Bankruptcy: A petition filed by certain credit grantors to have a debtor judged bankrupt. If the bankruptcy is granted, it is known as an involuntary bankruptcy.

Item-specific Statement: This offers an explanation about a particular trade or public record item on your report, and it displays with that item on the credit report.

Judgment Granted: The determination of a court upon matters submitted to it. A final determination of the rights of the parties involved in the lawsuit.

Loan: Something that is borrowed, especially a sum of money that is expected to be paid back with interest.

Last Reported: On a credit report, this is the date the creditor last reported information about the account.

Liability: The state of being responsible for something, especially by law.

Liability Amount: The amount for which you are legally obligated to a creditor.

Lien: A legal document used to create security interest on another's property. A lien is often given as security for the payment of a debt. A lien can be placed against a consumer for failure to pay the city, county, state or federal government money that is owed. It means that the consumer's property is being used as collateral during repayment of the money that is owed.

Line of Credit: In open-end credit, this is the maximum amount a borrower can draw upon or the maximum that an account can show as outstanding.

Location Number: The book and page number on which the item is filed in the court records.

MOP/Short for Manner of Payment: The way that a buyer chooses to compensate the seller of a good or service that is also acceptable to the seller.

Typical payment methods used in a modern business context include cash, checks, credit or debit cards, money orders, bank transfers and online payment services such as PayPal.

Non-Verification: When you cannot compare two or more items, or the use of supplementary tests, to ensure the accuracy, correctness, or truth of the information.

Notice of Results: If your investigation results in information being updated or deleted, you may request that the corrected information in your credit history be sent to eligible credit grantors and employers who reviewed your information within a specific period of time. If your investigation does not result in a change to your credit history, results will not be sent to other lenders.

Obsolescence: A term used to describe how long negative information should stay in a credit file before it's not relevant to the credit granting decision. The FCRA has determined the obsolescence period to be 10 years in the case of bankruptcy and 7 years in all other instances.

Unpaid tax liens may remain indefinitely, although Experian removes them after 15 years.

Original Amount: The original amount owed to a creditor.

Original Delinquency Date: The original delinquency date is the date an account first became delinquent and after which it was never again brought current.

Plaintiff: The person who brings a case against another in a court of law.

Primary User: This is the user that initially created the account. Primary users are able to edit their own information as well as the information of secondary users.

Payment Status: This reflects the previous history of the account, including any delinquencies or derogatory conditions occurring during the previous seven years (i.e., current account, delinquent 30, current was 60, redeemed repossession, charge-off – now paying, etc.).

Personal Information: Information on your personal credit report associated with your records that has been reported by you, your creditors and other sources. It may include name variations, your driver's license number, Social Security number variations, your date or year of birth, your spouse's name, your employers, your telephone numbers, and information about your residence.

Personal Statement: You may request that a general explanation about the information on your report be added to your report. The statement remains for two years and displays to anyone who reviews your credit information.

Petition: If a consumer files a bankruptcy but a judge has not yet ruled that it can proceed, it is known as bankruptcy petitioned.

Plaintiff: One who initially brings legal action against another (defendant) seeking a court decision.

Potentially Negative Items: Any potentially negative credit items or public records that may have an effect on your creditworthiness as viewed by creditors.

Repossession: Repossession is a process where an auto lender can take back possession of your vehicle, sometimes without warning you in advance or having permission from the court. Repossession typically occurs after you've become behind on your auto loan payments.

Recent Balance: The most recent balance owed on an account as reported by the creditor.

Recent Payment: The most recent amount paid on an account as reported by the creditor.

Released: This means that a lien has been satisfied in full.

Report Number: A number that uniquely identifies each personal Experian credit report. This number is displayed on your personal credit report and should always be referenced when you contact us.

Reported Since: On a credit report, this is the date the creditor started reporting the account to Experian.

Repossession: A creditor's taking possession of property pledged as collateral on a loan contract on which a borrower has fallen significantly behind in payments.

Request an Investigation: If you believe that information on your report is inaccurate, you must provide the sources of the information to check their records at no cost to you. Incorrect information will be corrected and information that cannot be verified will be deleted. Experian cannot remove accurate information. An investigation may take up to 30 days. When it is complete, you will receive the results.

Request for Your Credit History: When a credit grantor, direct marketer or potential employer makes a request for information from a consumer's credit report, an inquiry is shown on the report. Grantors only see credit inquiries generated by other grantors as a result of an application of some kind, while consumers see all listed inquiries including prescreened and direct marketing offers, as well as employment inquiries. According to the Fair Credit Reporting Act, credit grantors with a permissible purpose may inquire about your credit information prior to your consent. This section also includes the date of the inquiry and how long the inquiry will remain on your report.

Responsibility: This indicates who is responsible for an account; it can be single, joint, cosigner, etc.

Revolving Account: This is credit automatically available up to a predetermined maximum limit so long as a customer makes regular payments.

Risk Scoring Models: A numerical determination of a consumer's creditworthiness. This tool is used by credit grantors to predict the future payment behavior of a consumer.

Shared Account: An account with two people listed as owners.

Season Trade Line: This is a line of credit that the borrower has held open in good standing for a long period of time, typically at least 2 years. The "seasoned" part simply implies that the account is aged or that it has an established history.

Satisfied: If the consumer has paid all of the money the court says they owe, the public record item is satisfied.

Secured Credit: A loan for which some form of acceptable collateral, such as a house or automobile, has been pledged.

Security: Real or personal property that a borrower pledges for the term of a loan. Should the borrower fail to repay, the creditor may take ownership of the property by following legally mandated procedures.

Security Alert: A statement that is added once the credit bureaus are notified that a consumer may be a victim of fraud. It remains on file for 90 days and requests that a creditor get proof of identification before granting credit in that person's name.

Service Credit: Agreements with service providers. You receive goods such as electricity and services such as an apartment rental and a health club membership, with the agreement that you will pay for them each month. Your contract may require payments for a specific number of months, even if you stop the service.

Settle: Reaching an agreement with a lender to repay only part of the original debt.

Source: The business or organization that supplied certain information that appears on the credit report.

Status: On the credit report, this indicates the current status or state of the account.

Subscriber: A person who pays to receive or access a service.

Statute: A written law passed by a legislative body.

Trustee: An individual person or member of a board given control or powers of administration of property in trust with a legal obligation to administer it solely for the purposes specified.

Tax Form 12277: This is the tax screw-up that can destroy your credit. Form 12277 is the "Application for Withdrawal of Filed Form 668 (Y), Notice of Federal Tax Lien." It has been available to taxpayers for years, but originally the stipulations to withdraw a tax lien by the IRS were so stringent, few people ever succeeded.

Tax Lien: This is a lien imposed by law upon a property to secure the payment of taxes. A tax lien may be imposed for delinquent taxes owed on real property or personal property, or as a result of failure to pay income taxes or other taxes.

Terms: This refers to the debt repayment terms of your agreement with a creditor, such as 60 months, 48 months, etc.

Third-Party Collectors: Collectors who are under contract to collect debts for a credit department or credit company; collection agencies.

Tradeline: An entry by a credit grantor to a consumer's credit history maintained by a credit reporting agency. A tradeline describes the consumer's account status and activity. Tradeline information includes names of companies where the applicant has accounts, the dates accounts were opened, credit limits, types of accounts, balances owed and payment histories.

Transaction Fees: These are fees charged for certain usage of your credit line – for example, to get a cash advance from an ATM.

TransUnion: One of three national credit reporting agencies. The other two are Experian and Equifax.

Truth in Lending Act: Title I of the Consumer Protection Act; it requires that most categories of lenders disclose the annual interest rate, the total dollar cost and other terms of loans and credit sales.

Undesignated Account: In this case, no status was reported by the creditor reporting the account information.

Unsecured Credit: Credit for which no collateral has been pledged. Loans made under this arrangement are sometimes called signature loans; in other words, a loan is granted based only on the customer's word, through signing an agreement that the loan amount will be paid.

Vacated: This indicates a judgment that was rendered void or set aside.

Variable Rate: An annual percentage rate that may change over time as the prime lending rate varies or according to your contract with the lender.

Verification: The process of verifying whether data in a credit report is correct or not. It is initiated by consumers when they question some information in their file. Credit reporting agencies will accept authentic documentation from the consumer that will help in the verification.

Victim Statement: A statement that can be added to a consumer's credit report to alert credit grantors that a consumer's identification has been used fraudulently to obtain credit. The statement requests the credit grantor to contact the consumer by telephone before issuing credit. It remains on file for 7 years unless the consumer requests that it be removed.

Voluntary Bankruptcy: If a consumer files the bankruptcy on their own, it is known as voluntary bankruptcy.

Wage Assignment: A signed agreement by a buyer or borrower, permitting a creditor to collect a certain portion of the debtor's wages from an employer in the event of default.

Withdrawn: This means a decision was made not to pursue a bankruptcy, a lien, etc., after court documents have been filed.

Writ of Replevin: A legal document issued by a court authorizing repossession of security.

(Transunion , 2018) (Equifax, 2018) (Innovis, 2018) (Consumer Fraud Protection Agency , n.d.) (e-Oscar , 2018)

References

Check Systems . (2018). Retrieved from
https://www.chexsystems.com/web/chexsystems/co
nsumerdebit/page/home/!ut/p/z1/04_Sj9CPykssy0x
PLMnMz0vMAfIjo8ziDRxdHA1Ngg183AP83Qwc
XX39LIJDfYwM3M30wwkpiAJJ4wCOBkD9URA
lMBP8PUKMgCa4-
rgbG3kbugeaoCtAs8LAHKYAtyVe-
lHpOflJEP845iUZW6TrRxWlpqUWpRbplRYBhT
NKSgqKrVQNVA.

Consumer Fraud Protection Agency . (n.d.). Retrieved
from
https://duckduckgo.com/?q=consumer+fraud+prote
ction+agency&t=ffab&atb=v148-4b_&ia=web.

Consumer Protection Act . (2018). Retrieved from
https://www.consumerfinance.gov/.

Do Not Call List . (n.d.). Retrieved from
https://www.donotcall.gov/.

e-Oscar . (2018). Retrieved from http://www.e-oscar.org/.

Equifax. (2018). Retrieved from
https://www.equifax.com/personal/.

Experian . (2018). Retrieved from
https://www.experianplc.com/.

Federal Trade Commission. (n.d.). Retrieved from
https://www.ftc.gov/enforcement/rules/rulemaking-
regulatory-reform-proceedings/fair-debt-collection-
practices-act-text.

Federal Trade Commission . (2018). Retrieved from
https://www.ftc.gov/.

FICO . (2018). Retrieved from
https://ficoscore.com/education/#WhatYour.

Four Types of Credit . (2018). Retrieved from
creditcards.com.

Innovis. (2018). Retrieved from https://www.innovis.com/.

Transunion . (2018). Retrieved from
https://www.credit.com/credit-reports/credit-
bureau/transunion/.

United State Bancrupsy Court . (2018). Retrieved from
http://www.uscourts.gov/services-
forms/bankruptcy.

VantageScore . (2018). Retrieved from
https://your.vantagescore.com/interpret_scores.

Thank You!

Dr. Credit King
Chayo Briggs
chayobriggs.com
(800) 216-8871

www.ingramcontent.com/pod-product-compliance
Lightning Source LLC
Chambersburg PA
CBHW031430270326
41930CB00007B/640